W9-AEZ-212

Wallace Stevens: Words Chosen Out of Desire

Comment sic iennes colombia
en vng char q̃ fut riche et beau
manient venue en lost damõ
pour lui faire hastif secours

Wallace Stevens

Words Chosen Out of Desire

ぷ

BY HELEN VENDLER

THE UNIVERSITY OF TENNESSEE PRESS
KNOXVILLE

iii

Frontispiece: Venus and her Doves.
By permission of the British Museum.

Library of Congress Cataloging in Publication Data
Vendler, Helen Hennessy.
    Wallace Stevens: words chosen out of desire.
    Includes index.
    1. Stevens, Wallace, 1879–1955—Criticism and inter-
pretation—Addresses, essays, lectures. I. Title.
PS3537.T4753Z82   1984   811'.52   83-23588
ISBN 0-87049-427-9

ACKNOWLEDGMENTS

I am grateful to the Department of English at the University of Tennessee at Knoxville for the kind hospitality extended to me during my visit as Hodges lecturer, and especially to Professors John Fisher and B.J. Leggett, the best of hosts.

"Apollo's Harsher Songs: 'Desire without an object of desire,'" copyright © 1980 by Helen Vendler, is reprinted here by permission of the AWP *Newsletter*, May 1979.

Alfred A. Knopf, Inc., and Faber and Faber, Ltd., have kindly granted me permission to quote from the following works:

Opus Posthumous, by Wallace Stevens, edited by Samuel French Morse, copyright © 1957 by Knopf.

The Palm at the End of the Mind: Selected Poems and a Play, by Wallace Stevens, edited by Holly Stevens, copyright © 1971 by Knopf.

Letters of Wallace Stevens, edited by Holly Stevens, copyright © 1966 by Knopf.

The Collected Poems: The First Collected Edition, Wallace Stevens, copyright © 1954 by Knopf.

CONTENTS

Wallace Stevens: Words Chosen Out of Desire

INTRODUCTION

The chapters in this book, except for the first, were originally delivered in 1982 as the Hodges Lectures at the University of Tennessee at Knoxville. At the suggestion of Professor John Fisher, I took the occasion to think once again about Wallace Stevens. Though there are poets undeniably greater than Stevens, and poets whom I love as well, he is the poet whose poems I would have written had I been the poet he was. I would not have known it possible to have this peculiar standing with respect to a poet had I never come across Stevens' work. When I see Stevens misunderstood, as I believe he often is, I feel some obligation, in consequence, to present an alternative view; and these chapters are an attempt, through a glance at some of Stevens' shorter poems, to present the Stevens I know to the public eye, which still too often finds Stevens remote and distant from the common life. Perhaps one cannot be surprised at this: Stevens' self-presentation in poetry is not unlike his self-presentation in life.

The new "oral biography" of Stevens by Peter Brazeau, *Parts of a World: Wallace Stevens Remembered,* contains many tragicomic vignettes in which a friend or colleague of Stevens tries to read Stevens' poetry, only to retire baffled:

> Talking about his poetry, I said, "Mr. Stevens, I just can't understand your stuff. If I had to choose between you and Robert Service, I'd take Robert Service because I can understand Robert Service." He says, "Chawlie, it isn't necessary that you understand my poetry or any poetry. It's only necessary that the writer understand it. . . . I understand it; that's all that's necessary.[1]

To another acquaintance who asked him to explain a poem, Stevens said gnomically, "I don't think you'd understand this unless you wrote it."[2] Perhaps there is no better way of understanding Stevens than to imagine oneself writing the poem—to write it out as if it were an utterance of one's own. Eventually, as one writes the strange lines, it becomes clear why Stevens used to stay longest in the Klee galleries in the Museum of Modern Art:[3] Klee's childlike outliness and so-phisticated palette, his ironic humor and lyricism, share something with Stevens' poems. Klee would have understood Stevens' aphor-ism, "All poetry is experimental poetry" (*OP*, 161).[4]

If each poem is a new experiment, the ground on which it experiments is the past, both the past of the genre and the past of the *oeuvre*. I have given some examples here, for instance, of Stevens' reworking of Keats and of his re-using, over and over, his own image of the walker by the ocean. Nothing is more characteristic of Stevens than his restlessness ("It can never be satisfied, the mind, never"), unless it is his exquisiteness of response, a combination of receptivity and flinching that any reader of the poems soon learns to recognize. His perennial quick flush of vitality was as quickly followed by distaste; and that temperamental susceptibility gave him his fun-damental donnée—the disappointments of desire:

> Although the romantic is referred to, most often, in a pejorative sense, this sense attaches, or should attach, not to the romantic in general but to some phase of the romantic that has become stale. Just as there is always a romantic that is potent, so there is always a romantic that is impotent. (*OP*, 180)

Though the conceptual bases of Stevens' poems have been ably set out, and Stevens' intellectual and poetic sources are gradually being enumerated, the task of conveying the poems as something other than a collection of ideas still remains incomplete. "One reads poetry with one's nerves," said Stevens, and he added, "To read a poem should be an experience, like experiencing an act" (*OP*, 162, 164). To render what the nerves register and to trace the experience of a Stevens poem would tax anyone's best powers. In simplifying the poems (as all exposition must, if only by its linear detail), I have tried not to falsify them. I have wanted to read Stevens as he wanted to be read, as "a revelation of nature" (*OP*, 164) even though that nature be projected onto another plane, the plane of language. If it seems elementary to talk of the elements of life or "nature" that these poems treat, I do so for a reason. To say that one poem is about being reprieved from dying, another about a home wake, another about being American, another about resisting suicidal despair, another about envying the amnesia of nature, is only to remind readers that Stevens' poems concern the general emotional experiences common to us all. Perhaps only a lyric poet could say baldly that life is "not

4

people and scene but thought and feeling" and could urge that we "step boldly into man's interior world" (*OP*, 170), but that interior world, our construct of the world and all the world we have, is one of great vividness and reality. It is also one that changes radically over time as we age, so that the task of registering it is an unending one. And yet, even now, the distinguished critic John Bayley can refer to "the queer ghost world of Wallace Stevens."[5] If the solid object of realistic novels (Bloom's kidney is Bayley's example) had ever been the aim of lyric, one might take alarm. But the interior world of perception, emotion, and intellectual construction has always seemed, to lyric poets, the locus of reality. The volatility of the inner world is precisely the volatility of lyric. The stability of lyric, on the other hand, depends not on external objects but on the convergences and exigencies of achieved form. In the completed poem, motion is contained but remains motion. Summer's distillation, says Shakespeare of his sonnets, is "a liquid prisoner pent in walls of glass," and Stevens' version is that in the poem the world "will have stopped revolving except in crystal" (*Notes toward a Supreme Fiction*, "It must Give Pleasure," X). Some theories of reading emphasize the formed crystal; others the revolving (or the deconstructing) motion; in every poem it is possible to find both. In writing his poems, Stevens felt vividly the persistent querying and "decreation" of the fictive; in looking at the poems after the fact he preferred to remember the radiant moment when he had succeeded in calling the world by name. Two months before he died, Stevens inscribed a copy of his *Collected Poems* to his daughter's young English professor:

> Dear Elias: When I speak of the poem, or often when I speak of the poem, in this book, I mean not merely a literary form, but the brightest and most harmonious concept, or order, of life; and the references should be read with that in mind.[6]

Some of the poems considered here bear out that success in finding an adequate form, fully mobile and fully fixed, for a moment of interior life.

I think, with others, that Stevens' powers increased with age. The fiction we construct of a poet's "development" must be, of its nature, one containing many gaps; but insofar as such a fiction underlies this book, it would tell the story of a poet who had, from young manhood, great depth of feeling, but who discovered only gradually a restricted set of formal counters adequate to feeling and knowledge.

Stevens was a poet continually reworking, with great originality, his materials, intent on a precision so exact that only a formula like "Three-four cornered fragrances / From five-six cornered leaves" could represent what his over-acute senses took in *(An Ordinary Evening in New Haven,* VIII). He fought off persistent tendencies to the sentimental, the grandiose, and the transcendent. He exhibits, like most poets, a gradual passage from an aesthetic of the beautiful to an aesthetic of the arranged, one that can include the dissonant and the darkened, even the black violets of death (*Metaphor as Degeneration*).

It has been objected that a criticism suggesting that poems spring from life is reductive, that to say that *Le Monocle de Mon Oncle* is about Stevens' failed marriage is somehow injurious to the poem.[7] It seems to me normal to begin with the life-occasion as we deduce it from the poem; it is only an error when one ends there. To tether Stevens' poems to human feeling is at least to remove him from the "world of ghosts" where he is so often located, and to insist that he is a poet of more than epistemological questions alone.

Stevens' own explicit description of his project appears in the late poem *Local Objects,* unhappily omitted from *The Palm at the End of the Mind.* The poem is about objects in the world that are not domestic objects. Stevens was a man without a home; he made a home instead from the Elizabeth Park and the Connecticut River, those local objects. He had quarreled with his father when his father had objected to his choice of wife; he never saw his father again, and though he revisited his mother after his father's death, he had broken with his past in Reading, and remarked with regret on the dissociation he felt with the old life there.[8] Because the marriage had proved unhappy, he resigned himself to a future with no hope that things would improve in that *foyer* engendered by romance; in the poem, he uses that French word, with its suggestions of the domestic hearth, with bleak irony.

The local objects of Connecticut acted for Stevens as matrices in which, and through which, insights and integrations came, as he named and described these objects, over and over. He scarcely knew whether he did it to create them or to save them—all he knew was the persistence of the desire to contemplate them and write about them. The words chosen out of desire seemed to occur of themselves: and in the process of seeing and describing, the things themselves, the local objects, became not things alone but moments as well. This transformation of a spatial object into a temporal event is for Stevens the axis on which poetry turns. The world presented itself to him in visual terms; and yet poetry turned the visual object into the temporal integration, into that musical score for experience that we call a poem. The temporal unfolding of the moment becomes in its turn itself an aesthetic object, he realized—it becomes the classic, the beautiful, as the temporal event in words is re-spatialized into the serene poetic object, "an absolute foyer beyond romance." In no poem is Stevens' human loneliness more nakedly revealed; at the same time, in no poem do we know more acutely the intense satisfaction he felt when desire found names for his local objects:

Local Objects

He knew that he was a spirit without a foyer
And that, in his knowledge, local objects become
More precious than the most precious objects of home:

The local objects of a world without a foyer,
Without a remembered past, a present past,
Or a present future, hoped for in present hope,

Objects not present as a matter of course
On the dark side of the heavens or the bright,
In that sphere with so few objects of its own.

Little existed for him but the few things
For which a fresh name always occurred, as if
He wanted to make them, keep them from perishing,

The few things, the objects of insight, the integrations
Of feeling, the things that came of their own accord,
Because he desired without knowing quite what,

That were the moments of the classic, the beautiful.
These were that serene he had always been approaching
As toward an absolute foyer beyond romance. *(OP,* 111-12)

It must be remembered that before the poem put the local objects on paper, the page was blank. These objects were "not present as a matter of course," whether "on the dark side of the heavens or the bright," because they come into existence only insofar as they become, now, the virtual objects of language, though they were once the visual objects of sight. Stevens' deep attachment for his local world will I hope be more fully recognized as poems like *The River of*

Rivers in Connecticut and *The Hermitage at the Center* become better known. Of course his primary allegiance, like that of all poets, is to language and its possibilities.

In *Local Objects,* as in so many other poems, Stevens experiments with writing what might be called an algebraic statement into which each reader can substitute his own values for x and y (in this poem, one's own cause for a rupture with the past and one's own precious local objects). This sort of poetry was written before Stevens (notably by Dickinson) and has been written after him (especially by Ashbery). Stevens, and other such poets, presume that the experience under scrutiny is broad enough to be known to any reader; that any reader will have a renunciation by which to calibrate "Renunciation—is a piercing Virtue—" or a disappointment by which to ratify "The first year was like icing. / Then the cake started to show through" (Ashbery, *More Pleasant Adventures).*[9] Ashbery ironizes this algebraic generalization ("Heck, it's anybody's story, / A sentimental journey—'gonna take a sentimental journey' "), but that is his way of acknowledging his own origins in Dickinson and Stevens. To read these poets without a personal calibration, ratification, and substitution is to read them emptily.

Stevens presumes, then, that his deprivations and his desires are ours. In *Local Objects,* a poem written in old age, he recalls lines that he had written earlier, in *Notes toward a Supreme Fiction:*

> From this the poem springs: that we live in a place
> That is not our own and, much more, not ourselves
> And hard it is in spite of blazoned days.
>
> ("It Must Change," IV)

That was said elegiacally, in a dying fall. Now, although the counters are the same—loneliness and compensation—the emphasis has shifted to the value of the blazoned days. Stevens assumes that at some verge of life we all realize that we are spirits without a foyer in this world, and yet that some few things tether us to the world and give value to life—those objects for which a natural and fresh desire rises unbidden. This sentiment alone would not be interesting enough to maintain a poem; the poem needs the happening it enacts. In this happening, an estranged and impoverished sadness acquires by desire first a collection of objects, then a collection of names, then a recurrent refreshed motion of the spirit, a motion of wanting ("he wanted to make them, [he wanted] to keep them . . . / Because he desired"), then a collection of events ("moments of the classic, the beautiful"), then a place worth living for, "that serene he had always been approaching / As towards an absolute foyer beyond romance." The spirit without a foyer, by a series of happenings during the course of the poem, gains an absolute, if intermittent, foyer in desire and the words chosen out of desire.[10] In following the poem, we are reminded of the possibility of that journey in ourselves, of the recurrence of desire even in the absence of the romantic, even in the absence of a secure place, whether in the past or in the present, in this world. Stevens' austerity of language perhaps keeps his work from being a poetry for everyone, but it is not poetry for, or about, a world of ghosts. It springs from fact, and the trajectory it traces is one Stevens himself described:

> We leave fact and come back to it, come back to what we wanted fact to be, not to what it was, not to what it has too often remained. The poetry of a work of the imagination constantly illustrates the fundamental and endless struggle with fact.
> (Prose statement on the poetry of war, *Palm*, 206)

In following Stevens' excursions from the facts of his life into the projections of desire, and his perpetually original accommodations of desire to fact, I have hoped to show both his poetry of the human condition and his poetry of the English language.

1. APOLLO'S HARSHER SONGS
"Desire without an object of desire"

The words of Mercury," Armado says at the close of *Love's Labor's Lost,"* are harsh after the songs of Apollo." Apollo's songs, like those of Orpheus, are conventionally thought to be full "of linked sweetness long drawn out," but the criterion of sweetness or melodiousness has always been questioned by our greater poets. On the whole, Wallace Stevens is still considered one of the euphonious, "sweet," "aesthetic" poets, against whom the anthologies range our modern realists and ironists. There is some truth in the opposition, of course, or it would not have been made: *The Idea of Order at Key West* sounds different from *The Waste Land.* I choose here to enter Stevens' work by way of an interrogation of his harsher poems, those in which a brutality of thought or diction reveals feelings obscured by playfulness or obliqueness in his more decorative poems. I do this in part because I think the role of feeling in Stevens' poems has not yet been clarified. It is popularly believed that Stevens is a poet preoccupied by the relations between the imagination and reality, and there is good reason for the popular belief, since Stevens so often phrased his own preoccupation in those unrevealing words. The formula, properly understood, is not untrue; but we must ask what causes the imagination to be so painfully at odds with reality. The cause setting the two at odds is usually, in Stevens' case, passionate feeling, and not merely epistemological query.

One poem by which to enter this topic is *Chaos in Motion and Not in Motion* (1947); the title is itself unnerving as a violation of the axiom that a thing cannot be and not be in the same way at the same time:

> Oh, that this lashing wind was something more
> Than the spirit of Ludwig Richter . . .
> The rain is pouring down. It is July.
> There is lightning and the thickest thunder.

It is a spectacle. Scene 10 becomes 11,
In Series X, Act IV, et cetera.

People fall out of windows, trees tumble down,
Summer is changed to winter, the young grow old,
The air is full of children, statues, roofs
And snow. The theatre is spinning round,
Colliding with deaf-mute churches and optical trains.
The most massive sopranos are singing songs of scales.

And Ludwig Richter, turbulent Schlemihl,
Has lost the whole in which he was contained,

Knows desire without an object of desire,
All mind and violence and nothing felt.

He knows he has nothing more to think about,
Like the wind that lashes everything at once.[1]

The poem is composed of many reminiscences of former poems; it
treats its subject with a mixture of comedy, irony, pathos, and
brutality. I isolate Stevens' moments of brutality toward himself and
his life because brutality, in Stevens (and in other poets as well), is
usually a sign of extreme discomfort, misery, and self-hatred. Many
of Stevens' poems—read from one angle, most of the best poems—
spring from catastrophic disappointment, bitter solitude, or personal sadness. It is understandable that Stevens, a man of chilling reticence, should illustrate his suffering in its largest possible terms. That
practice does not obscure the nature of the suffering, which concerns
the collapse of early hopeful fantasies of love, companionship, success, and self-transformation. As self and beloved alike become, with
greater or lesser velocity, the final dwarfs of themselves, and as social
awareness diminishes dreams of self-transcendence, the poet sees
dream, hope, love, and trust—those activities of the most august
imagination—crippled, contradicted, dissolved, called into question, embittered. This history is the history of every intelligent and
receptive human creature, as the illimitable claims on existence made
by each one of us are checked, baffled, frustrated, and reproved—
whether by our own subsequent perceptions of their impossible
grandiosity, or by the accidents of fate and chance, or by our betrayal
of others, or by old age and its failures of capacity. In spite of the
severe impersonality of Stevens' style, in spite even of his (often
transparent) personae, it is himself of whom he writes. He has been
too little read as a poet of human misery.

11

The human problem—stated late but very baldly in *Chaos in Motion and Not in Motion*—is that its hero "Has lost the whole in which he was contained, / Knows desire without an object of desire, / All mind and violence and nothing felt." I do violence to these lines in detaching them from what precedes and follows them, but I do so for a reason. More often than not, the human pang in Stevens is secreted inconspicuously in the poem, instead of being announced in the title or in the opening lines. It is the usual, if mistaken, way of commentators to begin at the beginning and to take Stevens' metaphysical or epistemological prolegomena as the real subject of the poem, when in fact they are the late plural of the subject, whose early candor of desire reposes further down the page. And so I isolate what I take to be the psychological or human "beginning" of the poem, its point of origin in feeling, which, though it comes late in the poem, serves as the center from which the other lines radiate.

This center, which I have just quoted, tells us that the worst thing that can happen to a poet has happened to its hero: he has stopped having feelings. In Stevens' words, he is "all mind and violence and nothing felt." Since feeling—to use Wordsworthian terms—is the organizing principle of poetry (both narratively, insofar as poetry is a history of feeling, and structurally, insofar as poetry is a science or analysis of feeling), without feeling the world of the poet is a chaos. As we know, as the poet knows, the absence of feeling is itself—since the poet is still alive—a mask for feelings too powerful to make themselves felt: these manifest themselves in this poem as that paradoxical "desire without an object of desire," libido unfocused and therefore churning out in all directions—like a wind, as the last line of the poem says, "that lashes everything at once." Unfocused and chaotic libido does not provide a channel along which thought can move. Once there is an object of desire, the mind can exert all its familiar diversions—decoration, analysis, speculation, fantasy, drama, and so on. But with no beloved object, the mind is at loss; the hero of the poem has "lost the whole in which he was contained . . . / He knows he has nothing more to think about." The landscape is the objective correlative to this state of mind: "There is lightning and the thickest thunder."

The poem, as I have so far described it, ought to be a poem of *sturm und drang*, beset by the turbulent wind of desire, surrounded by its attendant *donner und blitzen*. But the brutality of the poem is that it treats its own problem with indifferent irony. The hero is "Ludwig Richter, turbulent Schlemihl," and his sufferings are watched through a monocle:

> It is a spectacle. Scene 10 becomes 11,
> In Series X, Act IV, et cetera.

This passage is a self-quotation from *Like Decorations in a Nigger Cemetery*, in which inception itself is satirized:

> An opening of portals when night ends,
> A running forward, arms stretched out as drilled.
> Act I, Scene I, at a German Staats-Oper.
> (XIX)

We all begin in the hope of romantic embrace: by the time *Chaos in Motion* is written we have moved on from Act I, Scene I, to the tenth series of performances in the Staats-Oper, and in that tenth series we are in the fourth act of some play, and in that fourth act we are moving from scene 10 to scene 11: in short, we are almost to Act V. And surely Series X is the last of the season. The poet has watched these operatic performances of desire too many times: like anyone middle-aged he has ceased to believe in the "running forward, arms stretched out"—but the wild thrashing of unfocused desire continues. It has preoccupied Stevens elsewhere; in *Puella Parvula*:

> Keep quiet in the heart, O wild bitch. O mind
> Gone wild, be what he tells you to be. *Puella.*

In *Chaos in Motion* Stevens quotes another early poem, the triumphant *Ploughing on Sunday*. There, while his docile neighbors troop off to church, the poet, violating the Sabbath, blasphemously harnesses his team to the plough and takes to the fields, full of indiscriminate joy in the sun and wind alike: in that poem, "the wind pours down," while now "the rain is pouring down." It is July, the month of credences of summer, when the plenitude of desire was felt in the past, and the mind could lay by its trouble. Now, in disbelief in the existence of any object of desire, the old seasonal myth of sun and love is abandoned, and with icy detachment Stevens enunciates all conceivable tragedies as though they could be watched with ultimate *froideur:* suicide, "people fall out of windows"; the decay of nature, "trees tumble down"; the ice age, "summer is changed to winter"; decline, "the young grow old"; violation of natural process in a

13

chaotic upheaval of life and art, "the air is full of children, statues, roofs / And snow." The *theatrum mundi* itself collapses, its fall coincident with the collapse of its impotent institutions and its stage scenery: "The theatre is spinning round, / Colliding with deaf-mute churches and optical trains." In this Götterdäm merung, harmony itself is reduced to elemental monotony: "The most massive sopranos are singing songs of scales."

All of this is normally material for elegy, and most of it has been or will be material for elegy in Stevens:

> The last leaf that is going to fall has fallen.
> She is exhausted and a little old.
> The general was rubbish in the end.
> A cabin stands, deserted, on a beach.

A roof abandoned, a statue broken, a leafless tree, a fall of rain, a beloved grown old, a church of bird-nest arches and of rain-stained vaults, a theater or capitol collapsing—all can elicit lament, and do, except when Stevens is being brutal. In *Chaos in Motion* the unbearable acceleration and offhand inventory of the spectacle—"People fall out of windows, trees tumble down, / Summer is changed to winter, the young grow old"—borrows a common cinematic brutality (used in film for comic effect)—to reproduce the look of the *theatrum mundi* to the eyes of the old, who have seen the cycle too many times repeated. The old seraph in *Notes* has seen too many springs:

> The Italian girls wore jonquils in their hair
> And these the seraph saw, had seen long since,
> In the bandeaux of the mothers, would see again.

The seraph has gone though his own cycles of seraphic chastity and Saturnalian desire (when he turns to a satyr): he has desired the mothers and the daughters alike and has turned from both in surfeit and disbelief. Even in spring, the world, to this jaded Stevens, seems "a withered scene."

Stevens' grand claim on us in his later poems is his willingness to refuse lyric emotions. The truth is, he tells us, that the old detach themselves from empathy and, with a certain weary sense of déjà vu, see their grandchildren predictably rising to adolescent erotic idolatry and entrusting themselves to Summer's warmth, only, in their turn, to encounter failure, loss, cold, age, and death. One greets this spectacle, in middle age, without the tragic emotions with which one passed through the cycle oneself. And yet there is no diminution in desire: there is only a loss of belief in a possible object adequate to desire. The tonelessness with which Stevens recounts the disastrous events around him is meant to reflect his own sense of inevitable and repetitive human fate. And yet tonelessness is the ultimate lyric risk. The reader who can penetrate irony, brutality, rapidity, and toneless-ness to see behind them a catastrophic loss of feeling, a fear of unleashed libido with no conceivable object, and the despair of a mind of genius that has nothing more to think about, will read *Chaos in Motion and Not in Motion* as a poem reflecting one of the fundamental miseries of the old.

The brutality of style I have dwelt on in *Chaos in Motion* has early roots in Stevens, but when it appears in *Harmonium* it is usually preceded or followed by some softening of perception. Two cases exhibiting this softening must suffice: in *Anecdote of the Prince of Peacocks* Stevens meets his own potential madness; in *The Apostrophe to Vincentine* he meets the unaccommodated object of desire before she has been clothed in the beauty of fantasy. Each poem is distanced by being given a rhetorical title—*Anecdote of, Apostrophe to*—so that, even though they are, unusually for Stevens, written in the first person, they scarcely share at all in the lyric convention of personal experience. The poet—here, the Prince of Peacocks, full of showiness and *superbia*—meets the Saxon-named Berserk: he meets him in the realm of poetry—sleep and moonlight. But Berserk is "sharp as the sleepless," a phrase suggesting that if the Prince of Peacocks should wake into the dread sunlight of experience, he would go mad. The impossibility of the poet's evading Berserk, even in dreams, is the purport of the colloquy between the two. When the poet asks, "Why are you red / In this milky blue? . . . / Why sun-colored, / As if awake / In the midst of sleep?" Berserk answers that he sets his traps in the midst of dreams, forcing the poet to recognize the hazards of mentality even in the kingdoms of escape. At this point in the poem the diction turns brutal:

> I knew from this
> That the blue ground
> Was full of blocks
> And blocking steel.

However, Stevens' retreat from brutality into incantation is immediate:

> I knew the dread
> Of the bushy plain
> And the beauty
> Of the moonlight
> Falling there,
> Falling
> As sleep falls
> In the innocent air.

This is an unrewarding ending to a poem which began so promisingly as an exploration of the threats—reaching even to breakdown—posed by consciousness.

The Apostrophe to Vincentine is a bolder poem. The female, imagined naked, is nothing more to her poet than a lean, small, white, nameless animal, dwarfed by the magnitude of the scale of earth and sky. Nevertheless, the poem allows her to preexist this reductive imagining. She is already, in the poet's mind, Heavenly Vincentine; he is already enamored. Still, he engages in the deliberate aesthetic exercise of depriving her of all interiority and humanness and exterior garments, trying to see her as a purely visual object, an isolated biological phenomenon. This peculiar exercise prefigures Stevens' later enterprises of viewing the ding-an-sich. But it is one thing to try to see the sun or a March morning without evasion; to see the Platonic beloved in this way is in itself deeply repellent to Stevens. Melodramatically he affixes Roman numerals to each stage of Vincentine's appearance. Number I, though reserving the final repellency—animality—for later, otherwise presents the unadorned female figure in pure visuality:

> I figured you as nude between
> Monotonous earth and dark blue sky.
> It made you seem so small and lean
> And nameless
> Heavenly Vincentine.

In II, Vincentine is allowed warmth (that is to say, her poet is allowed to see her as flesh, not only as outline). She is given a dress to wear, a modified green (like that worn by the spring "queen . . . in slipper green") to contrast with the monotonous earth and dark blue sky. She is also given hair (as a modified brunette). Peculiarly, her other

attribute besides warmth is cleanliness; one suspects the exigencies of
rhyme:

> I saw you then, as warm as flesh,
> Brunette,
> But yet not too brunette,
> As warm, as clean
> Your dress was green,
> Was whited green,
> Green Vincentine.

In III, Vincentine is allowed, so to speak, a soul, exhibited in her
independent motion; she is also placed in a society, so that her voice
can be heard and so that she can express feeling:

> Then you came walking,
> In a group
> Of human others,
> Voluble.
> Yes: you came walking,
> Vincentine.
> Yes: you came talking.

In her progressive assumption of human attributes as she
approaches the poet, Vincentine changes from a tiny animal outline
in the cosmic scale to a living woman, around whom the cosmos falls
into place. She becomes in fact the heavenly or Platonic axis on which
all creation turns, rendering monotonous earth no longer monotonous but rather a place imbued with her reality. Or so we believe
when the fourth stanza begins:

> And what I knew you felt
> Came then.
> Monotonous earth I saw become
> Illimitable spheres of you.

This transformatory rhetoric generally leaves behind the original
dwarfed state and leads to the language of apotheosis. Stevens, after
accomplishing the apotheosis of earth, refuses to remain on the level
of the glorified and re-does his apotheosis twice more, each time
reiterating Vincentine's original state of nude leanness, but making
her, as she was not at the beginning, a "white animal," in the uneasy
phrase, "that white animal, so lean":

> Monotonous earth I saw become
> Illimitable spheres of you
> And that white animal, so lean,

> Turned Vincentine,
> Turned heavenly Vincentine,
> And that white animal, so lean,
> Turned heavenly, heavenly Vincentine.

Brutality and apotheosis end in a stalemate. We remember Vincentine at least as powerfully in her repellent incarnation as a white animal so lean as in her named and transfigured state, brunette, dressed, walking, talking, and feeling. The poem shows us a mind willing and welcoming the decor of thought and fancy, while unable to rid itself of primal reductivenss and visual disgust. The reductive diction, telling us in itself that poetry and apotheosis are *not* one, but remain in a problematic relation, marks the speaker as a man caught between the nameless lean, on the one hand, and illimitable spheres of the beloved, on the other. There is no diction equally appropriate to both.

In an altogether harsher poem from *Harmonium,* Stevens subjects his own idealizations to ridicule. *The Virgin Carrying a Lantern,* an unsettling poem with a Pre-Raphaelite title, embodies Stevens' brutality in the negress who watches malevolently the more seraphic and elegiac postures of life and supposes "things false and wrong" about "the lantern of the beauty / Who walks there." The poem pretends to ally itself unequivocally in its declarations with the innocent virgin:

> There are no bears among the roses,
> Only a negress who supposes
> Things false and wrong
>
> About the lantern of the beauty
> Who walks there, as a farewell duty,
> Walks long and long.
>
> The pity that her pious egress
> Should fill the vigil of a negress
> With heat so strong!

The simpering Victorian voice, reproving the negress' suppositions as "false and wrong," expressing indignation at the negress' strong "heat" ("The pity" of it!), and endorsing the "pious egress" of the virgin, is entirely contradicted by the brutal left-hand side, so to speak, of Stevens' diptych: if the negress supposes bears, it is because she is acquainted with bears, while the virgin knows only roses; the negress is in the dark, the virgin bears a lantern; the negress, with her strong "heat," is sexual, the virgin chaste; the negress an impious spy, the virgin a pious vestal. The trouble with the virgin's universe, which would be pleasing if it contained only roses, dutiful virgins, lanterns, and pious farewells, is that it contains the negress, her vigil, her heat, and her suppositions. The negress makes the virgin ridiculous; no one engaged in a "pious egress" can ever be poetically respectable. The negress' heat has the last word. The poem may be seen as a rewriting of Blake's lamb and tiger: the virgin is what Melville would have called a radiant ninny, but there is none of Blake's admiration for his tiger embodied in Stevens' figure for the dark, for the heated, and for the bestial in himself.

These earliest examples from *Harmonium*—Berserk, the animal Vincentine, and the negress—show Stevens already aware of certain incompatibilities—between waking and dreaming, between the animal and the heavenly, between chaste piety and strong heat—against which his only defenses were a comic or ironic language, a rhetorical distance in entitling, a reduction of the lyric potential of the "I" who speaks, and, most of all, a rather tedious polar separation of imagery: the milky blue of moonlight opposed to the red of sunlight, the small animal Vincentine contrasted to the illimitable heavenly Vincentine, the pious virgin distinguished from the heated negress. Crispin thought placatingly that his life could be a voyaging "up and down between two elements," but the ranker element in *The Comedian* is described with too little of the brutality that honesty would dictate; instead, Stevens treats it with the same unchanged high rhetoric that is the vehicle for all of Crispin's experience. Crispin is not made sufficiently unhappy by the tension between his two elements: Berserk, who comes summoned by Stevens' incapacity to mediate between sun and moon, never invades *The Comedian*.

If we turn our attention to the shape of Stevens' whole career, we can see three large phases in his management of this problem. (I would take *Chaos in Motion* as the harsh turning point between the second and third phases.) The first phase, represented by the poems I have instanced from *Harmonium*, resorted to certain concealments of tension, on the one hand, and to violent dislocations of sensibility, on the other. Both were attempts at accommodation, and brought Stevens to the state of misery in which he met the traditionally invulnerable Berserk, his traps, and his blocking steel.

19

The second phase finds Stevens attempting to exorcise these private tensions by resorting to a solution in the social order. As he tries to see depression as a social, rather than a personal, emotion, he thinks it may be ended by social cohesion rather than by interior resolution. An early example of a poem that goes wrong—though the number of these is legion among the war poems—is *The Men That Are Falling*. This poem begins wonderfully, in private loss, as the moon "burns in the mind on lost remembrances." As the poet leans on his bed, he realizes that the pull he feels to it is not the pull of sleepiness, but of desire:

> This is not sleep. This is desire.
>
> Ah! Yes, desire . . . this leaning on his bed,
> This leaning on his elbows on his bed,
>
> Staring, at midnight, at the pillow that is black
> In the catastrophic room . . . beyond despair,
>
> Like an intenser instinct. What is it he desires?

Some confrontation with the erotic lost remembrances evoked by the empty pillow where the beloved should lie is in order, but Stevens places instead an imagined head, a male one, on the pillow—"the head of one of the men that are falling," in part a double of himself, in part his opposite. A flicker of brutality is allowed to enter in the description of the iconic head, "thick-lipped from riot and rebellious cries," but the soldier is redeemed from the subhuman by the "immaculate syllables / That he spoke only by doing what he did." Stevens thinks to turn his attention here to those moral "words" of heroic action "that are life's voluble utterance," insisting that right action alone is the arena for the resolution of inner pain. But by turning the acts of soldiers into a form of utterance, he suggests that his own "immaculate syllables" spring as well from a form of death, symbolized by the absence of the inamorata on the pillow. Having died to her, he rises into syllables. The impotence he characteristically evokes in misery is "cured" in this poem by the dangerous example of the hero, always a seductive icon for Stevens. Just as he had tried in *Harmonium* for a euphony symbolized in the *Infanta Marina*, binding together nature, thought, and art, so in *Parts of a World* he imagines a synthesis among flying birds, marching soldiers, and rolling drums—the motions of nature, the motions of social action, and the motions of the music of war. The consequent self-effacement represents the effacement of the psychic problem of private misery, and the poet's aversion from the corresponding aesthetic problem of the relation of that misery to both art and nature. The oppositions between euphony and cacophony, harmony and eccentricity, the seraphic and the satiric are in Stevens symbols for the discrepancy between the irresistible yearnings of desire and the irreversible misery at its failure. But the war poems turn the symbolic focus outward; as a result, they become forced.

In the notion, developed in several middle poems, of a contradictory plurality of "truths," Stevens began to solve conceptually the problem of the conflict between desire and loss. But the conceptual concession to plurality did not in itself invent a style representative of the several truths of appetite and failure. The evasions inherent in retaining an old style for new perceptions can be seen in the poem most clearly articulating the creed of plural truths, *On the Road Home*:

> It was when I said,
> "There is no such thing as the truth,"
> That the grapes seemed fatter.
> The fox ran out of his hole.
>
> You ... You said,
> "There are many truths,
> But they are not parts of a truth."
> Then the tree, at night, began to change.

The two figures "said we stood alone." The man in *Anglais Mort à Florence* had stood at last "by God's help and the police," but here God and social institutions have disappeared. The narrator continues, in an argument against the Logos:

> "Words are not forms of a single word.
> In the sum of the parts, there are only the parts.
> The world must be measured by eye."

The "you" replies with a comparable indictment of idolatry:

> "The idols have seen lots of poverty,
> Snakes and gold and lice,
> But not the truth."

These sentiments are all very well; they are anti-Platonic, nominalist, iconoclastic. The poem asserts that the expression of such dry sentiments enhances nature:

> It was at that time that the silence was largest
> And longest, the night was roundest,
> The fragrance of the autumn warmest,
> Closest and strongest.

The "rhyming" superlatives here suggest a Platonic extension and extrapolation of nature, as well as a Platonic coherence of the parts of nature; this extension, extrapolation, and coherence represent Stevens' unresolved wish that the sum of the parts should be more than the parts. Brutality of language ought to appear in coincidence with the absence of Platonic reassurance; in this poem the nominalist theme is not allowed its appropriate style of closure.

It is one of Stevens' claims to greatness that he went on to invent a new style—the style of parts as parts, of words refusing to form a single word, of the many truths not part of "a" truth, the style of many of the most interesting late poems. For Stevens, one theoretical problem in inventing such a style lay in the suspicion that it would call metaphor into question. Metaphor implies analogy and resemblance, neither of which can be stable in a world of nonce effects. In *Harmonium* Stevens had decided, in *Metaphors of a Magnifico,* to distinguish between fact (twenty men crossing a bridge into a village), distinctive individual experience (twenty men crossing twenty bridges into twenty villages), and collective perception (in which the twenty men become one man):

> Twenty men crossing a bridge,
> Into a village,
> Are twenty men crossing twenty bridges,
> Into twenty villages,
> Or one man
> Crossing a single bridge into a village.
>
> This is an old song
> That will not declare itself . . . .

Brute fact, in the second essay at the rendering of this sight, seems to win the upper hand: "Twenty men crossing a bridge / Into a village / Are / Twenty men crossing a bridge / Into a village." However, all speculation about the truths occurring on the far side of the copula is vanquished, finally, by the sensuous particulars of the scene, as the Magnifico ceases to be a philosopher of perception, ceases even to be a spectator, and becomes a participant:

22

> The boots of the men clump
> On the boards of the bridge.
> The first white wall of the village
> Rises through fruit-trees.
>
> Of what was it I was thinking?
> So the meaning escapes.
>
> The first white wall of the village . . .
> The fruit trees. . . .

At one point the Magnifico's view had been as "certain as meaning," but in the sensual experience, "the meaning escapes." These separations between speculation and experience are still present in the absolute disjunction between the dispute on truth and the fat grapes of *On the Road Home.*

The most strictly comparable poem in the later work to *Metaphors of a Magnifico* and *On the Road Home* is *The Motive for Metaphor,* a poem in which the interpenetration of thought (with its consequent vocabulary of words, things, metaphor, expression, obscurity, motive, and so on) and sense (with *its* vocabulary of seasonal change, colors, moonlight, trees, clouds, and birds) is almost except for the ending, complete. The partial truths, earlier so eagerly embraced as a solution for the absence of authority, now rightly take on the impoverished colors appropriate to them, instead of nostalgically imitating, in Platonic superlatives, the very consolations they were meant to forgo.

The degree of self-loathing Stevens felt in sacrificing his absolutist "Platonic" self—that which believed, with all an acolyte's sincerity, in religion, love, and art—is evident in the self-contempt at the beginning of *The Motive for Metaphor* with which he addresses his new, "partial" self:

> You like it under the trees in autumn
> Because everything is half dead.
> The wind moves like a cripple among the leaves
> And repeats words without meaning.
>
> In the same way, you were happy in spring,
> With the half colors of quarter-things,
> The slightly brighter sky, the melting clouds,
> The single bird, the obscure moon—

> The obscure moon lighting an obscure world
> Of things that would never be quite expressed,
> Where you yourself were never quite yourself
> And did not want nor have to be,
>
> Desiring the exhilarations of changes:
> The motive for metaphor, shrinking from
> The weight of primary noon,
> The ABC of being,
>
> The ruddy temper, the hammer
> Of red and blue, the hard sound—
> Steel against intimation—the sharp flash,
> The vital, arrogant, fatal, dominant X.

Whatever voice it is that speaks here, it speaks dismissively of the poet's love of half colors and quarter-things. He loves half-dead things in autumn and quarter-things in spring, the voice says, because such things represent change: a half-dead thing can die, a cripple was once healthy, a moon can wax and wane, a single bird can become a chorus, a cloud can melt, a sky can brighten. Spring and autumn are the seasons of change. But the speaking voice detests those exhilarations of changes which are the motive for metaphor. This new, self-contemptuous voice which opens *The Motive for Metaphor* sees the seductiveness of change as an evasion of the obdurate, blocking, trapping knowledge of the fatal and dominant self, the self that, under all the changes, one is. That is the self that the sharp light of noon, without any shadows, would reveal. It is at once the ABC of being and also its X, the Alpha and Omega of self, that which the Prince of Peacocks had been afraid to face—Berserk and his traps of steel. In moonlight, says the self-accuser in *The Motive for Metaphor,* "you yourself were never quite yourself / And did not want nor have to be." You shrank from the weight of primary noon. But the speaker knows, now, with entire intimacy, "the hard sound— / Steel against intimation—the sharp flash / The vital, arrogant, fatal, dominant X." That steel is both vital and fatal, ABC and X, the infant self and its later hierophant. This is a very brutal poem, in which Stevens is much unkinder to his younger self than he will be in his last poems. But it is a relief, after earlier evasions, to hear him being so harsh.

The final hammer and knife-blade, the smith's hammer and the executioner's edge, are extremely beautiful, but just slightly overdone. The speaker has not yet been wooed entirely away from his more shrouded and nuanced haunts, in spite of his sortie into a contemptuous tone. The trouble with biding in autumn and spring after they no longer mediate adequate self-knowledge is that the words one writes about them cease to have any meaning, and the divine afflatus is crippled. Stevens—it is part of his greatness—was quick to see when he was being false and, in spite of the immense stubbornness of his slow nature, was willing to force himself unwillingly on to the next stage of discovery, even if it meant new desolation. *The Motive for Metaphor* finds him falling back on the natural ground of his own life and private misery, rather than looking toward the social order for a collective example of ethical escape. The misery in *The Motive for Metaphor* lies in the pain of the choices it offers: a crippled, half-dead, and meaningless life in autumn (it being now no longer possible to return to spring) or a submission to what one shrinks from: a brutal solar weight, a hard hammer, the surgical flash of the fatal X. Stevens dreads being exposed to that sun, being tempered by that hammer, finding that blocking steel against his intimations (though he no longer believes he will go mad under the trial, as he did when he was the Prince of Peacocks). With the dread there coexists a compelling attraction—the exhilaration of a new sort of self-knowledge, a change into the changelessness of a final, permanent self. Because the new phase incorporates the motive for all the previous ones, the desire for change (which is the motive for metaphor), it attracts. But the poem implies that the new self-knowledge that it implicitly recommends will be the last possible phase, the fatal phase, and therefore the end of poetry. This suspicion causes both the nostalgia for previous seasons of happiness, no matter how evasive, which the poem candidly exhibits, and the desire for the new.

Stevens' style in *The Motive for Metaphor* is, comparatively speaking, one of apparent simplicity. But the old Platonism, the desire for harmony, is smuggled in by way of two flurries of apposition, at the middle and end of the poem. Apposition is a figure which of itself implies that things can be aligned in meaningful parallels, that metaphorical equivalences are a portion of significance—that

> the weight of primary noon
> the ABC of being

> the ruddy temper
> the hammer of red and blue
> the hard sound
> steel against intimation
> the sharp flash
> the vital, arrogant, fatal, dominant X

can all be substituted, one for the other, to signify a dreadful exposure from which the earlier, more fugitive poet, shrinks. In this parallelism Stevens betrays his nostalgia for synthesis and system: brutality has extended to his self-perception and to his imagery without yet having reached his syntax. *Chaos in Motion and Not in Motion* extends this brutality to syntax, letting that crippled wind fully loose, allowing it to lash everything at once, changing the self-loathing of *The Motive for Metaphor* to self-irony, refusing soothing syntax in favor of rapid primary syntactical forms.

In his last years Stevens writes a poetry of powerful retrospective weight in which all the attitudes exhibited and assumed over a long life are admitted to the arena, each seen as something authentic in its time. The worst bitternesses, when they recur, as they do even in *The Rock*, subside. Brutality appears, and recedes. In the great and heartbreaking poem of self-evaluation, *Things of August*, Stevens forgives all his selves, remembers all of them, accedes to the unintelligibility of the world, and celebrates the new text of it he has created. He is now, as he will say in *The Rock*, the "silent rhapsodist" of the earth. Of all the poems I could choose to show the last stage of Stevens' harshness, I will turn to one about sexual feeling in old age, called *The Dove in Spring*:

> Brooder, brooder, deep beneath its walls—
> A small howling of the dove
> Makes something of the little there,
>
> The little and the dark, and that
> In which it is and that in which
> It is established. There the dove
>
> Makes this small howling, like a thought
> That howls in the mind or like a man
> Who keeps seeking out his identity
>
> In that which is and is established . . . It howls
> Of the great sizes of an outer bush
> And the great misery of the doubt of it.

Of stripes of silver that are strips
Like slits across a space, a place
And state of being large and light.
There is this bubbling before the sun,
This howling at one's ear, too far
For daylight and too near for sleep.

The dove is Venus' bird, its absence mourned earlier in *Harmonium*, in *Depression before Spring*, when, though the cock has crowed, "ki-ki-ri-ki / Brings no rou-cou, No rou-cou-cou," and "no queen comes / In slipper green." It is the "tempestuous bird," the "dove in the belly" who "builds his nest and coos" when things of the world appear promising and bright. It is the dove that rises up every spring when the Italian girls wear jonquils in their hair. Stevens is seventy-four as he writes this poem, his last word almost on the persistence of desire. What is one to make of the voice of Venus' dove at seventy-four? Hatred, irony, and comedy can appear in the literature of sexual meditation in old age; one thinks of Yeats. But Stevens' meditation is entirely respectful and serious; he does not feel absurd or reprehensible for harboring the dove; what he feels is a sadness for the dove and for himself. The dove is imprisoned behind walls, in the dark. It can no longer coo; it can only howl. A howl is its singing, and it decides to sing even an unlovely song, rather than fall silent. The dove knows that somewhere outside there is a great bush that is its natural habitat; at the same time, it doubts that any such bush exists. This doubt causes its misery: it howls of "a place and state of being large and light," but all it has of that light is what it perceives in slits through its prison bars, in stripes of silver.[2] The dove's small howling takes place at night. It prevents sleep, without presaging a new day. Spring's infuriations, the poem tells us, are never over. They take, in old age, forms that may seem degenerate—a dove displaced from a bough to a prison, a dove that does not coo but howls, a dove that cannot any longer see the undulating silver fans of any imaginable mate—but if truth is to be told, even degenerate forms must be allowed their pathos of expression.

I do not mean to sentimentalize Stevens in insisting that his poems are meditations on emotions of love, idolatry, loss, self-loathing, and self-forgiveness. He is so chaste in self-revelation that his emotions are easily passed over. A poem like *The Dove in Spring*, written in "the little and the dark," sees the sexual impulse, and all the love and idealization it gave rise to in life, as strictly parallel to the impulse to thought and the impulse to self-definition. In allowing a syntactic parallelism between these three impulses—the sexual, the intellectual, and the personal—Stevens is resorting not to Platonism but to memory, the memory of how his life had structured itself around three persistent shapings of identity. The grief of the ending of the poem is not the elegiac sorrow for the great bush or the large light state, but rather the grief of Tithonus, that one can neither die nor live, as one endures the last protests and affirmations of desire.

James Merrill once remarked in a *Paris Review* interview that Stevens "continues to persuade us of having had a private life, despite—or thanks to—all the bizarreness of his vocabulary and idiom." On the whole, criticism has avoided the evidences of that private life, but it is, as Merrill says, so inseparable from the incomparable style invented to express it that it is a failure of imagination to discuss the style without its subject. The lapses and failures of idealization—especially the idealization of romantic love, forced on us by nature, culture, and, above all, literature—press Stevens to an ever more stringent, and even harsh, analysis of the interrelation of emotion's flights and their eventual correction in time. It may be that the harshness or brutality which I have been describing is Stevens' defense against a Romantic sweetness, though I think not. It is rather, I feel sure, the expression of an anger that a mind so designed for adoration never found adoration and sensuality compatible; they remained locked compartments, a source of emotional confusion and bitterness. In the end, however, Stevens' unwillingness to abandon either of his two incompatible truths—the truth of desire and the truth of the failure of desire—led to a great amplitude of human vision not granted to those who live more comfortably in body and soul, and to a truth-telling ease not granted to those who have fewer difficulties to confess.

2. DESIRE
"The lover, the believer, and the poet"

Shakespeare's Theseus speaks with some distrust of those men who "are of imagination all compact," who give to "airy nothing / A local habitation and a name."[1] Theseus says it is the lunatic, the lover, and the poet who do this: Stevens changes Theseus' grouping slightly, and says it is the lover, the *believer*, and the poet. These, he continues, are the clairvoyant men, whose "words are chosen out of their desire" (*A Primitive Like an Orb*, IV). We are all, throughout our lives, lovers and believers; in Stevens' eyes that means we are all poets of what he called the poetry of the idea. Anyone who singles out, by desire, some one man or woman as a singular valued object, creates by that act a fiction, an idealized image in which desire finds, or thinks to find, its satisfaction. Anyone who has ever believed in a cause or in a God creates in the same way an idealized image—the perfect state, the Messiah, Paradise—which is also one of those supreme fictions, a Platonic form. Desire always expends itself on imagining "the fulfillment of fulfillments, in opulent / Last terms" (*Primitive*, IV). But it is not only our sexual and religious desire that imagines the existence of an ideal object; it is also our intellectual desire, hungry for an ideal truth, that is, a complete and stable one. Remarks on the Beautiful, the Good, and the True have usually emphasized the ultimately stable forms of these Platonic entities in a transcendent world where (as in Keats) Beauty is Truth, Truth Beauty, or (as in Spenser) Heavenly Love and Heavenly Beauty are one in Christ. Stevens, however, shifts the locus of attention away from the transcendent to the actual, from the object of desire to desire inventing its object; and, most centrally, to the change over time of the desired object. We are betrayed by our investiture of the beloved object with all the qualities of perfection; and both romantic disillusion and the loss of religious faith put into question, for Stevens, the original desires which led us to sexual illusion and religious belief. Stevens is one of the last of our writers to experience fully the nineteenth-century crisis of the death of God; and he learned from Shelley and Coleridge the connection of the loss of religious faith with the loss of sexual faith. By linking the poet to the lover and the believer, Stevens aligns the skeptical crisis of aesthetic desire for the beautiful to the more familiar skepticisms attacking religious and sexual fidelity; and since his conception of the aesthetic includes a strong intellectual component, an epistemological crisis is linked, for him, to the aesthetic one.

For Stevens to be a lover is to write (he was thinking here of his letters and poems to his wife before they married); to be a poet is to speak *sotto voce,* mumbling to oneself; to be a believer is to listen to the word of God; to be a painter is to see. He himself is all four—a writer, a mumbler, a listener, a seer (a lover, a believer, a poet, and a painter):

> That's it. The lover writes, the believer hears,
> The poet mumbles and the painter sees,
> Each one, his fated eccentricity.
>
> (*Primitive,* XII)

Each one of these selves is wrenched from the perfect Platonic orbit by the eccentric planetary motion of desire, that force that moves all things. Desire, for Stevens, is always savage and always fierce: to look into one's own heart, to come home to oneself, is to start anew each time at the ground zero of desire:

> . . . Home
> Was a return to birth, a being born
> Again in the savagest severity,
> Desiring fiercely, the child of a mother fierce
> In his body, fiercer in his mind, merciless
> To accomplish the truth in his intelligence.
>
> (*Esthétique du Mal,* X)

Stevens is the poet of this overmastering and mercilessly renewed desire. Each moment of reflection, for him, is a rebirth of impulse toward fulfillment, as desire reaches for its object—sexual, religious, epistemological, or (encompassing them all) aesthetic. Hunger, for Stevens, is our eternal condition: famished for fulfillment, we achieve it uncertainly and not for long, but radiantly nonetheless. When that moment comes "of bright & blue birds & the gala sun" (as the title of one poem calls it), we "pronounce joy like a word of our own," and "we are joyously ourselves," as if there were "a gaiety that is being, not merely knowing / The will to be and to be total in belief / Provoking a laughter, an agreement, by surprise." The price of this ecstatic moment—which may be any newness in vision, in love, in insight, in political or religious conviction—is the destruction of the old illusions—romantic, intellectual, or historical—that had preceded the new one. "The mind . . . / to find what will suffice, / Destroys romantic tenements / Of rose and ice" (*Man and Bottle*). But the old delusion was itself once one of the fresh joys, and no one since Shelley has felt so strongly as Stevens the perpetual vanishing before us of objects of desire and the reformulating energy of the ever-desiring self. To create the new we must first de-create the old; and the reality of decreation (as Stevens called it, borrowing the word from Simone Weil) is as strong as the reality of creation. It is for this reason that Penelope's web becomes for Stevens the very image of human desire: woven afresh every day, it is unraveled again every evening; and each exhilaration of possession is followed by the despair of disbelief. "The powerful mirror of our wish and will" (*Poem with Rhythms*) is forever showing us a new illusion. In the end, desire is indistinguishable from despair, once we have understood the endlessness of its quest. Coleridge, who wrote the seminal poem of this theme, which he called *Constancy to an Ideal Object*, protects his ignorant protagonist, the woodman, from the knowledge that the phantom he pursues is one created in the fog by his own shadow. In the figure of the enraptured rustic, Coleridge shows us the ardor of all pursuit; in his own skeptical language, he shows us the mind which has realized the fictionality of all supreme fictions. "Such thou art," Coleridge says, addressing the Ideal Object,

> as when
> The woodman winding westward up the glen
> At wintry dawn, where o'er the sheep-track's maze
> The viewless snow-mist weaves a glist'ning haze,
> Sees full before him, gliding without tread,
> An image with a glory round its head;
> The enamoured rustic worships its fair hues,
> Nor knows he makes the shadow, he pursues![2]

Desire, its illusions and its despairs, is Stevens' great subject. Another way to put it is to say that the human illusions engendered by desire are his great subject. We are helpless, he sees, in this matter.

It is not possible for us to be without desire; we cannot help but engage in that process that Freudians call idealization and trace to Oedipal causes. Our common names for idealization are romantic love, religious belief, and political engagement: these do not differ in essence, for Stevens, from the poet's creation of the aesthetic object of desire. All human beings engage in poesis in constituting an imagined world to live in; and the engagement in poesis is coterminous with life. To be alive is to desire:

> The priest desires. The philosopher desires.
> And not to have is the beginning of desire.
> To have what is not is its ancient cycle.
> It is desire at the end of winter, when
>
> It observes the effortless weather turning blue
> And sees the myosotis on its bush.
> Being virile, it hears the calendar hymn.
>
> It knows that what it has is what is not
> And throws it away like a thing of another time,
> As morning throws off stale moonlight and shabby sleep.
>
> (Notes Toward a Supreme Fiction, "It Must be
> Abstract," II)

I pause here to ask how it can be thought that the poet who wrote the lines I have been quoting can be so often called "cold and cerebral" or "abstract" or "remote" or "finicky." Stevens is a genuinely misunderstood poet, it seems to me, in the world at large; he is rarely called a passionate writer, or a poet of ecstatic or despairing moments—and yet that is what he is. He is often a despairing lover, blaming himself for the failure in love, blaming his wife as well, and finally, in *The Rock,* blaming only the biological necessity that brings men and women together; he is a believer, like Santayana, without a faith, and his tonality, if not his substance, echoes the tones of English devotional verse; he is certainly not the dandy or the hedonist that Yvor Winters, who began the denigration of Stevens, took him to be.

Stevens has himself told us how he wanted us, as his posterity, to think of him. He certainly never dreamed he would be thought a hedonistic or dandiacal or aloof ancestor. On the contrary. If we want to see what he considered his own legacy to us, how he wanted to be remembered, we have to look at his two bequest-poems, *A Postcard from the Volcano* and *The Planet on the Table.* In the first of these,

Stevens imagines himself to be like one of the citizens of Pompeii buried beneath the lava of Mount Etna. Centuries after that explosion, we, the children of a later culture, come gathering flowers on the slopes of the volcano, never dreaming—or, rather, concealing from ourselves—that we too will feel an explosion one day, that death will bury us too in dust. We have an interval, as Pater said, and only an interval: we are largely unconscious, in our interval of strolling on the volcano or eating the concupiscent curds in the kitchen, of the incipient lava under our feet or the corpse in the back room. We are also unconscious, for the most part, of the cultural inheritance that has shaped our present consciousness. We feel and conceive the world as we do (and not as Hindus or Japanese do) because of our predecessors, those under the dust. We scarcely recall their existence; only, sometimes, when we see a ruined mansion, now shuttered, we recall that someone once lived there, that there was a moment when the mansion was inhabited. That *belle époque* has vanished except to the extent that we are its dependent heirs. Under the opulent sun, every order decays; and the sun gilds, or blooms with rosy hue, or smears with gold the cultural vestiges of each ruined former era. Stevens, speaking for the poets of his era, tells us (the children newly come) how our very language and perceptions stem from him; and how what he said of the world has become part of what we know as the world. We know "what he felt at what he saw."

Stevens begins this poem in the first person plural, speaking for all his fellow poets as well as for himself; but he ends in the singular, speaking of himself in the third person as the person who once lived in the mansion, leaving behind as his legacy to us the history of his desire, our sense that he was "a spirit storming in blank walls." His world has been gutted, his mansion is only a dirty and tattered shadow of itself; but the spirit persists in its vivid storms of desire and distress, and the opulent sun, undisturbed, shines on:

A Postcard from the Volcano

Children picking up our bones
Will never know that these were once
As quick as foxes on the hill;

And that in autumn, when the grapes
Made sharp air sharper by their smell
These had a being, breathing frost;

And least will guess that with our bones
We left much more, left what still is
The look of things, left what we felt

At what we saw. The spring clouds blow
Above the shuttered mansion-house,
Beyond our gate and the windy sky

Cries out a literate despair.
We knew for long the mansion's look
And what we said of it became

A part of what it is . . . Children,
Still weaving budded aureoles,
Will speak our speech and never know,

Will say of the mansion that it seems
As if he that lived there left behind
A spirit storming in blank walls,

A dirty house in a gutted world,
A tatter of shadows peaked to white,
Smeared with the gold of the opulent sun.

Harold Beaver, an English critic of American literature, has said that Stevens gives off "a Watteau-like air of picnicking in a rococo landscape."[3] But this is no picnic; it is a *voix d'outre-tombe*. It is the posthumous voice of that storming spirit, acting as spokesman for its fellow-spirits and their legacy to us. It could not be said more simply. The poem makes a statement and then utters a reprise of that statement: "Children picking up our bones" is taken up anew by "Children . . . weaving budded aureoles." The poem finds the simplest of equivalents for all its conceptual concerns: death is the explosion of the ground under our feet; the end of our era is the shuttering of the mansion we lived in; a cultural legacy is the poets' leaving behind what they felt at what they saw, and what they said of the mansion. The past is autumn; the present is the children's spring. Our ancestors had bodies quick as foxes, senses that breathed the smell of grapes, feelings that sprang from their senses, words that issued from their feelings. Inception becomes "budded aureoles"; conclusion is "literate despair." The end of a cultural epoch is the decline of the great mansion to a dirty house in a gutted world. The persistence of nature is the opulent sun. But the inability of the vital sun to resurrect the life inside the vacated mansion appears in the sun's external effect: it can only smear its gold on the outside of the dirty house (an effect borrowed from Shakespeare's sonnets via Keats's ode *To Autumn*, as the sun gilding pale streams becomes the occluded sun touching the stubble fields with rosy hue). Stevens' continuing wish to write with the utmost simplicity, and to reach us, his posterity, with his spirit still storming on the blank pages of his book is nowhere clearer than in this parable of pastness. His stylized universe is made up of the barest and simplest equivalents he can find to symbolize the death of one culture and the beginning of a new culture unconsciously dependent on the old one. Self-deprecatingly, Stevens calls his poem a postcard. It says, not "Wish you were here," but "Soon you will be here, as I am"—and reminds us of the obligation of each generation to leave, in utterance, a memorial of what it felt at what it saw, to leave a vestige of its "spirit storming." Nothing could be simpler, more direct, more intimate, more benevolently ironic toward the children weaving budded aureoles.

To write in a posthumous voice means to make the supreme imaginative act of imagining oneself dead, one's desires ended, one's record of utterance of feeling complete, one's structures of feeling obsolete and gutted. The strange peace of the poem comes from that cessation of all desire, but we see the trace of the bitterness of the still-living author of the poem in his vision of his own life and desiring spirit degenerated to that empty and dirty house in a gutted world, that body once quick as foxes—his own—now turned to a shade, its mortal dress a tatter of shadows, its flesh calcined to the whiteness of bones. The literate despair at extinction, suppressed in the initial benevolent legacy to the beautiful young, finds expression in the revenge at the sun, its gold radiance denigrated to a ruining smear. In this way, the truth of Stevens' own pang at death is preserved in the midst of his posthumous prophecy.

The other final testamentary view of desire and its aftermath in utterance comes to us in the poem *The Planet on the Table*, written (though this can only be conjectured) after Stevens completed for Knopf the manuscript version of the *Collected Poems*. Stevens sees his life's work contained in a single object, the potential book lying before him on a table: each page reminds him of a moment of intense feeling, something in the past, something he has loved. In a poem contemporary with *The Planet on the Table*, and written also about his life's work, Stevens wonders whether, as a person who has lived for art, he is a skeleton, all geometrical armature and no flesh. But he reassures himself by paging through his printed works and recalling, in brief, the poems called *Someone Puts a Pineapple Together*, *Examination of the Hero in Time of War*, and *Credences of Summer:*

> Today's character is not
> A skeleton out of its cabinet. Nor am I.
>
> That poem about the pineapple, the one
> About the mind as never satisfied,
>
> The one about the credible hero, the one
> About summer, are not what skeletons think about.
>
> *(As You Leave the Room)*

And yet, the very fact that Stevens himself must ask,

> I wonder, have I lived a skeleton's life,
> As a disbeliever in reality,
>
> A countryman of all the bones in the world?

means that he anticipated the accusations that would be made by some readers—accusations of his inhumanity, bloodlessness, dryness, and cerebral abstraction. He felt in himself a difference from Keats, in short—and he had to explain that difference to himself.

Stevens saw that he conceived of himself as a poet of winter—of the moment when illusion has ceased—whereas Keats was a poet of spring, summer, and autumn, the seasons of growth and harvesting. Though he did write *Credences of Summer*, Stevens' most congenial seasons ranged from October through March, the seasons succeeding to Keats's stubble fields. In Stevens' autumn, a cold wind chills the beach, and the northern lights, with their fiery cold sublimity, have replaced the sun as illumination. In his region November, things are dead; as a snow man, he inhabits the January moment when one listens and beholds, but can utter nothing; later, he discovers "at the antipodes of poetry, dark winter," that there exists a Keatsian hint of inception and possible utterance, "the cricket of summer forming itself out of ice" *(A Discovery of Thought);* still later, he sees that the natural world (and he is included, even reluctantly, given the apathy of old age, in that world), inevitably begins its almost invisible spring life—the first fly, the "babyishness of forsythia," "the spook and makings of the nude magnolia," the comic turn after the tragic burial.

36

In short, Stevens' most authentic insights are those of a minimal-
ist poet; his art is, he realizes, fully as laden with feeling as that of any
other poet (and therefore not fleshless and skeletal); but the feelings
are often the powerful wintry feelings of apathy, reduction, naked-
ness, and doubt. Reassured that he is not a skeleton after all, he looks
at his manuscript *Collected Poems* as it lies on his table, and speaks
an epigraph for it as an epitaph for himself. In his twenties, he had
written an early poem in which he called himself Caliban (and his
"spectre" Ariel);[4] the name was chosen, we may conjecture, partly
out of sexual guilt and partly out of dismay at his always heavy and
ungainly appearance; never did any poet have a body more unlike his
soul. But now, in his seventies and already unwell from the fatal
disease that was to be diagnosed six months later (*L*, 856,881),[5] he
gave himself, for the first time (instead of self-deprecating names like
Professor Eucalyptus—meaning "well-concealed"—or Canon
Aspirin), the name appropriate to his ethereal soul, and called himself Ariel, the airy spirit trapped in an earthly prison.

When he asked himself, "What does seeing my *Collected Poems*
lying on the table seem like to me?" he remembered his days as a child
in school, and the terrestrial globe on the teacher's desk. That globe
represented the whole planet, though in miniaturized form—here is
Africa, here is the tropical zone, here is the North Pole. Art, too,
miniaturizes—but in its anagogical form it represents the whole
world as the poet has known it. His book is for him the planet on the
table. He bequeaths it to us—a poor reduction, perhaps, of the
affluence of life, but nonetheless permanent, as the organic life of the
larger planet, its trees and shrubs, cannot be. Wordsworth believed
that the works of mighty poets become part of the sum of reality;
Stevens is remembering that claim as well as Keats's remark that "if
Poetry comes not as naturally as the Leaves to a tree, it had better
not come at all" (To Reynolds, 27 February 1818). In short, a poem
is as much a natural product as a tree or shrub; and when we enter
our earthly existence, we find poems—Wordsworth's poems,
Keats's poems, Stevens' poems—present around us, as materially
visible as trees and mountains are. They too, our poems, are products
of that solar energy that makes all things come into being. Our
artificial distinctions between "nature" and "art" err: in this view,

art is part of nature. With deliberate simplicity, Stevens tells us what he thought his poems represented, as he leafed through them: they were "of a remembered time / Or of something seen that he liked." If we allow for Stevens' characteristic understatement, we might say that his poems preserved for him moments too valuable to be left unmemorialized, things too deeply loved to be left unsketched. These memories of place and time, memories of affinity, are a witness to the character of the greater planet of which they are a part:

The Planet on the Table

Ariel was glad he had written his poems.
They were of a remembered time
Or of something seen that he liked.

Other makings of the sun
Were waste and welter
And the ripe shrub writhed.

His self and the sun were one
And his poems, although makings of his self,
Were no less makings of the sun.

It was not important that they survive.
What mattered was that they should bear
Some lineament or character,

Some affluence, if only half-perceived,
In the poverty of their words,
Of the planet of which they were part.

The vast central boast in this poem, almost lost in the general reticence and understatement of its wording, is the claim, "His self and the sun were one" (a later version of "Divinity must live within herself" from *Sunday Morning*, but phrased as truth, not wish). Once again, in this text, Stevens takes as his method a reductive and parabolic simplicity: the earth is the great planet, his book is the little planet of the school; the energy of the universe is the sun; and all organic life is "the makings of the sun" typified in "the ripe shrub." It is not a Keatsian ripeness that Stevens claims for his poems: ripeness, he says, writhes and withers. It is something far more destitute—the poverty of words; and yet something resolute and permanent. His art exhibits a Roman strictness, exhibiting a "lineament," a "character" of the earth. It delineates; it characterizes. It does not, in the Keatsian manner, enact; rather, it offers a map with zones and poles of experience marked out on the fluid continuum of perception and desire. It shares with Wordsworth a Latin stoicism; it recollects the savagery and fierceness of desire, yet it recollects them in austere inquiry.

It is this severity, perhaps, which makes the poems seem cold to those readers who come with other expectations, whether of Keatsian luxury or Shelleyan exclamation. Stevens' poems are often second-order reflections on the stormings of first-order sensation. They are distillations. "The attar from the Rose," said Dickinson, "Be not expressed by Suns—alone— / It is the gift of Screws." "Essential Oils—are wrung."[6] It is only after Stevens' fierceness of desire has finished its initial storming into despair that its essence is expressed in the poems, in those exquisite reductions to simplicity that I have been quoting. "It was not important that they survive," Stevens said of his poems—and for him it was not important. What mattered to him was the writing of them, to track for himself the metamorphoses of plenary desire into wasted despair and its re-arousal into affluent desire again—that recurrent and unbiddable cycle.

At times the cycle seemed to him unbearable: "Why should the bee recapture a lost blague?"—"The old—old sophistries of June," as Dickinson called them.[7] But to be alive is to be susceptible to desire, to want the new influx of being, "The booming and booming of the new-come bee" *(Notes toward a Supreme Fiction,* "It Must Change," II). Shortly before he was hospitalized for cancer, Stevens wrote to one correspondent, "Easter is the most sparkling of all fêtes since it brings back not only the sun but all the works of the sun, including those works of the spirit that are specifically what might be called Spring-works: the renewed force of the desire to live and to be part of life" *(L,* 879). There is an echo here, in this spring letter, of the language of *The Planet on the Table:* "works of the sun" is a version of "makings of the sun." The valediction implicit in speaking of oneself in the past tense—"Ariel was glad he had written his poems"—gives the poem its extraordinary moving power; a few weeks later, in the last letter *(L,* 890) printed in the *Collected Letters,* Stevens wrote "I can neither concentrate on poetry nor enjoy poetry."

I have drawn this very broad picture of a very subtle poet because I believe it needs to be said, in the broadest way, that Stevens is our great poet of the inexhaustible and exhausting cycle of desire and despair. It should not be necessary to say aloud a truth which seems to me so self-evident. But it is clearly not self-evident to the world of readers, since Stevens was a private and reticent man, not a confessional poet. In the next chapter, I want to take up the question of Stevens' secrecies, the stylized ways he found to put his life of emotions into speech. But here I want to emphasize just the opposite, his explicitness—his constant use of entirely explicit emotional words like "savage," "fierce," "merciless," "despair," "storming," "desire," and so on. These are not the words of a cold, indifferent, or tepid mind; they are not the words of a dandy or a hedonist. They are the words of a poet, subject, in his solitude, to onslaughts of feeling that he could compare only to sidereal events like the flare of the aurora borealis, that destructive force sweeping away illusion. Otherwise put, he constantly felt "form gulping after formlessness"—as in the desiring heart and mind of the artist every formed object and image hungers for another object, another deceptive shadowy image in Plato's cave:

> Another wriggling out of the egg,
> Another image at the end of the cave,
> Another bodiless for the body's slough.
> *(The Auroras of Autumn)*

In Stevens' great hymn to destruction and decreation, *The Auroras of Autumn*, life is finally seen as changing color "to no end / Except the lavishing of itself in change." Our desire stays alive only by obliterating former objects of desire:

> It leaps through us, through all our heaven leaps,
> Extinguishing our planets, one by one,
> Leaving, of where we were and looked, of where
>
> We knew each other and of each other thought,
> A shivering residue, chilled and foregone,
> Except for that crown and mystical cabala.
> *(The Auroras of Autumn, VII)*

That crown and mystical cabala is desire itself, the flashing and ever-changing auroras.

Stevens' meditations on the restlessness of the soul, the heart, and the mind are the most unsparing account in poetry of the oscillations of skepticism and faith (if we take those words in their widest meaning). Never was there a more devout believer—in love, in the transcendent, in truth, in poetry—than Stevens. And never was there a more corrosive disbeliever—disillusioned in love, deprived of religious belief, and rejecting in disgust at their credulousness the "trash" of previous poems (as he says in *The Man on the Dump*). Always "merciless to accomplish the truth in his intelligence," Stevens re-examined his premises anew in every poem; and almost every poem describes yet again, from another vantage-point, the intractable appetite of desire, willing happiness for itself and thereby inviting unhappiness. Almost every poem examines, yet once more, that external world of mere being which offers so much on which to inscribe our idealizations, so much in which to find our objects of desire. There are times when nothing suits, of course, especially in old age:

> What I want more than anything else in music, painting and poetry, in life and in belief is the thrill that I experienced once in all the things that no longer thrill me at all. I am like a man in a grocery store that is sick and tired of raisins and oyster crackers and who nevertheless is overwhelmed by appetite. (*L*, 604, 23 June 1948)

Stevens wrote those words when he was sixty-seven, and we may see in them an echo of the poem written three years earlier, *Chaos in Motion and Not in Motion,* in which the protagonist knows "desire without an object of desire / All mind and violence and nothing felt."

In his last reduction and miniaturizing of the world of mere being, Stevens represents it by a few counters he had used twenty years earlier in *Some Friends from Pascagoula.* We are in the tropics, the realm of the sun; there is a palm tree; in the palm there is a bird with feathers of gold, the sun's color; the bird sings; its feathers shine in the fire of the sun; the wind moves slowly in the branches:

Of Mere Being

The palm at the end of the mind,
Beyond the last thought, rises
In the bronze decor,

A gold-feathered bird
Sings in the palm, without human meaning,
Without human feeling, a foreign song.

You know then that it is not the reason
That makes us happy or unhappy.
The bird sings. Its feathers shine.

> The palm stands on the edge of space.
> The wind moves slowly in the branches.
> The bird's fire-fangled feathers dangle down.

This iconic world, bronzed to permanence, is of course a tropical and stylized version of the *locus amoenus,* the beautiful place of desire: the palm, the sun, the gold bird, the wind, the sun-bronzed decor, and the song are a hard-edged Floridian version of the softer European *topos* of grove, bird, breeze, and carol. This is the desired world of the "higher" or "theoretical" senses, eye and ear, reified. There is something in it for seeing and hearing alike, though not for those "lower" senses, taste and touch. Though I have called the reduction of the world of desire to a bird singing in a tree a process of miniaturization (and it is), it is also, paradoxically, a process of aggrandizement: the single iconic form expands to fill the whole world, and so takes on the "total grandeur of a total edifice, / Chosen by an inquisitor of structures / For himself *(To an Old Philosopher in Rome).* Gauguin and Matisse both knew the strategic value of such simplification of forms, and knew the monumentality that forms acquire when thus simplified.

Stevens' ultimate word on the claims of sensual desire against the reasoning mind appears in the declaration which holds a dominant place in the absolute center of this late poem:

> It is not the reason
> That makes us happy or unhappy.

This axiom might seem too obvious to be stated except that for Stevens the primacy of desire was a truth that went against his upbringing and his education; perhaps it is a truth that needed, for him, to be re-won against internal resistance over and over. The foreign song of the sensual earth will always need to have human meaning and human feeling added to it by those fictions of intelligibility and desire we all project upon it. But the will to utterance and to constructive form is always solicited anew by the enigmatic appearances of the world; they create horizons for us at the end of the mind, on the edge of space. From them we make the internalized permanencies of gold and bronze which, for us, stand for the unknowable world of the beautiful, eternal, and inhuman sun.

All that I have said about Stevens' relation to desire could equally well be said of many other poets. In one of Coleridge's notebooks there is a summary phrase that condenses the relation between the mind and desire into a distillation; Coleridge observes

> The still rising Desire still baffling the bitter Experience, the bitter Experience still following the gratified Desire.[8]

The story of this tireless cycle is not a new one; but Stevens has not always been recognized as a participant in it, in spite of his own clear statements that he is. Of course his way of stylizing the oscillations between gratified desire and bitter experience is his own. I have spoken of his strategy of reduction to simplest counters, which is at the same time a strategy of monumentality. In my next chapter, on Stevens' secrecies, I will address his most individual stylization, the turn toward the impersonal lyric. And finally, in my fourth chapter, I will come to the teleology of the Stevensian lyric, its desire for perfection, its debate on orders of magnitude.

3. STEVENS' SECRECIES
"The obscurest as, the distant was"

I have called this chapter
"Stevens' Secrecies" because many of Stevens' strategies for freshness and originality are strategies of concealment, chiefly concealment of the lyric "I." Though these strategies conceal nothing from
the reader long used to Stevens' privacy, they are a stumbling-block
to the occasional reader, one who knows Stevens only from anthologies. There are four simple recommendations for a neophyte de-
ciphering Stevens. The first is to substitute "I" whenever Stevens says
"he" or "she": for "Divinity must live within herself," read "Divinity must live within myself," and so on. Second, never trust begin-
nings in Stevens; the emotional heart of a lyric by Stevens is likely to
be found in the middle of the poem: "Complacencies of the peignoir"
is less the emotional heart of the matter (though it is close to the
linguistic center) than "Death is the mother of beauty." Third, look
for the context of the poem, both in Stevens' whole canon and in his
poetic predecessors. Fourth, mistrust titles: *Anecdote of Canna* is not
about flowers and *The Snow Man* is not about a snow man; the bird
with the coppery, keen claws is not to be found in any aviary. Not
many poets would call a poem about their middle age and romantic
disillusion *Le Monocle de Mon Oncle.* These four recommendations
are all pedagogical and provisional ones. They need to be followed
by a fifth: When you have seen the heart of the emotional drama,
reconstituted the lyric "I," gotten past the obliquity of the opening
lines, and translated the odd title, then you must *undo* all you have
done, and read the poem afresh, relishing the oddness of the title,
reading without irritability the quirky beginning, resting in the fiction of "the anecdote of" or "two tales of" or "the sense of" or
"credences of" or "notes toward," savoring the reticence of the
poem's allusiveness. In short, you must repossess the poem as it exists
on the page in all its originality and strangeness.

These recommendations are only indicative; in fact, Stevens' secrecies are many and various, and are always a source of aesthetic delight to him—and, eventually, to us. I want to consider here four of Stevens' characteristic secrecies: the secrecy of allusion (for which my examples will be *Anecdote of the Jar* and *The Snow Man*); the secrecy of narrative (for which my example will be *The Emperor of Ice Cream*); the secrecy of symbol (for which I will take up *The Dove in the Belly*); and the secrecy of metaphysics (for which I use *The Hermitage at the Center*). These secrecies are all strategies of implication. Though Stevens enjoyed being a discursive poet, and expatiating grandly on great questions (as he does in the early sequences and in *The Idea of Order at Key West,* for instance) his greatest originality, I believe, always lay in his more hidden forms of utterance, where his eccentricity (the base of his design) is more strongly felt than in the poems of pronouncement, even such noble ones as the poem on Santayana.

Anecdote of the Jar, as various critics have seen, is a commentary on Keats's *Ode on a Grecian Urn.* Though this is nowhere said by Stevens, the poem is not comprehensible, in matter or manner, unless it is taken to be centrally about Keats's poem. Or rather, it alludes to Keats's poem as a way of discussing the predicament of the American artist, who cannot feel confidently the possessor, as Keats felt, of the Western cultural tradition. Where Keats had London, the British Museum, and an Hellenic urn, the American poet has Tennessee, a slovenly wilderness, and a gray stoneware jar. Where Keats had cultural and legendary ornamentation, the American poet has a bare surface:

> I placed a jar in Tennessee,
> And round it was, upon a hill.
> It made the slovenly wilderness
> Surround that hill.
>
> The wilderness rose up to it,
> And sprawled around, no longer wild.
> The jar was round upon the ground
> And tall and of a port in air.
>
> It took dominion everywhere.
> The jar was gray and bare.
> It did not give of bird or bush,
> Like nothing else in Tennessee.

The poem is a revoicing of the complaint of James (one of the chief influences on Stevens) about the poverty of the American scene, and the consequent danger of thinness in American art. The language of the poem deliberately reflects the absurdity of the American artist's attempt to write a lyric: shall he use language imported from Europe ("of a port in air," "to give of") or "plain American that cats and dogs can read" (as Marianne Moore put it) like "The jar was round upon the ground"? The poem keeps trying to write itself in inherited stanzas and showing us that it cannot, wrecking each proposed stanza form as it goes along, not only destroying its tetrameters with trimeters and pentameters, but failing to find any rhyme for "hill" except itself, abandoning its first notion of alternate rhymes for no rhyme at all, then deciding to rhyme three lines in a row ("air," "everywhere," "bare"). The American poet cannot, Stevens implies, adopt Keats's serenely purposive use of matching stanzas drawn from sonnet practice. Stevens was entirely capable, as we know from *Sunday Morning,* of writing memorable Keatsian lines and stanzas; so we must read the *Anecdote of the Jar* as a palinode—a vow to stop imitating Keats and seek a native American language that will not take the wild out of the wilderness. The humor of the ridiculous stanzas and the equally ridiculous scenario of the *Anecdote* does not eliminate an awkward sublimity in the jar; nor does it eliminate the rueful pathos of the closing lines.

Unlike *Anecdote of the Jar, The Snow Man* is comprehensible in itself, and does not betray, by outrageous peculiarities of language of the sort found in *The Jar,* an internal struggle for an appropriate language (though its French "to regard" is a minor instance of the same struggle). But we understand *The Snow Man* better, I think, when we see it as Stevens' answer to Keats's challenge voiced in the small impersonal poem, *In Drear-Nighted December:*

In drear-nighted December,
    Too happy, happy tree,
Thy branches ne'er remember
    Their green felicity—
The north cannot undo them
With a sleety whistle through them,
Nor frozen thawings glue them
    From budding at the prime.

Keats then considers the brook which with a sweet forgetting never "pets" about the frozen time; finally, he concludes with the wish that we could imitate the forgetting of nature and live in the present, not feeling the pang of past joy:

> Ah! would 'twere so with many
> A gentle girl and boy—
> But were there ever any
> Writh'd not of passèd joy?
> The feel of not to feel it,
> When there is none to heal it,
> Nor numbèd sense to steel it,
> Was never said in rhyme.[1]

Writhing, or not writhing, over passed joy is what *The Snow Man* is about. Stevens here attempts the amnesia of nature, an impossible task. Borrowing Keats's phrase "not to feel," Stevens changes it into "not to think"; and he decides to accept Keats's challenge and try to say "in rhyme" "the feel of not to feel it." The attempt to numb, while not annihilating, the senses—to continue to see and hear without admitting misery and loss—creates the structure of Stevens' poem:

> One must have a mind of winter
> To regard the frost and the boughs
> Of the pinetrees crusted with snow;
>
> And have been cold a long time
> To behold the junipers shagged with ice,
> The spruces rough in the distant glitter
>
> Of the January sun; and not to think
> Of any misery in the sound of the wind,
> In the sound of a few leaves,
>
> Which is the sound of the land
> Full of the same wind
> That is blowing in the same bare place
>
> For the listener, who listens in the snow,
> And, nothing himself, beholds
> Nothing that is not there and the nothing that is.

Stevens' turn from regarding to listening, from the visual to the aural, is borrowed from Keats as well, from the ode *To Autumn;* Stevens' continuation of the figure, as he executes a counterturn from listening back to beholding, "corrects" Keats's assumption that the essence of poetry is the utterance of a stream of sound, and suggests that for Stevens looking and hearing, imagery and musicality, occupy equal ground in the conception of lyric.

We can see one reason for Stevens' liking for the impersonal as a strategy in lyric (or as a secrecy of lyric) by reflecting on the impossibility of rewriting *In Drear-nighted December* in the first-person singular; Keats too knew the advantage here (and in his autumn ode) of suppressing the lyric "I." Stevens "corrects" Keats again here by making the trees in his own poem evergreens, not deciduous trees— trees that have the same plenitude in winter as in summer. Stevens gives his pines and junipers in fact a double foliage in winter, as snow and ice encrust and shag their full branches; and he "corrects" Keats once more by placing his trees not in a dreary night in the closing month of the year but in the glitter of the sun in the month beginning the new year. "Thou hast thy beauty too," says the poet to winter, thereby going the ode *To Autumn* one better. Stevens' title tells us, on the other hand, that we would have to cease to be flesh and blood and become men of snow in order to contemplate passed joy without writhing. Here, too, he writes to correct Keats, who had written of the four seasons in the mind of man, adding, "He hath his winter too of pale misfeature, / Or else he would forget his mortal nature."[2] Stevens suggests, correctively, that if we adopt the mind of winter we must indeed forget our mortal nature and numb our senses to the zero degree of the snow man. Stevens had so absorbed Keats that Keats acted in his mind as a perpendicular from which he constructed his own oblique poems: what we see as a secrecy of allusion was for Stevens no secrecy but rather an exfoliation of a continuing inner dialogue with Keats. Stevens' allusions, in his briefer poems, are more often to content than to language. If Keats says "tree," Stevens will say "pinetrees," "junipers," "spruces." If Keats says "the north . . . with a sleety whistle," Stevens will say "the sound of the wind." And if Keats says "crystal fretting" and "frozen time," of ice, Stevens will say "frost," "snow," "ice." If Keats says "not to feel," Stevens says "not to think."

There is yet another secrecy in *The Snow Man,* its concealing of progress in its series of self-embedding clauses. This special form, which we encounter also in *Domination of Black,* offers a syntactic version of the series of receding planes with which we are familiar in painting. We are not to think of any misery "in the sound of the wind, in the sound of a few leaves, which is the sound of the land full of the same wind that is blowing in the same bare place for the listener." The brilliantly visualized ice-shagged and snow-covered trees of the poem occupy a glittering foreground—almost an obstacle—through which we are made to pass, via the etherealizing and impalpable sound of the wind, to the fallen leaves, thence to the land, thence to the wind in a bare place, and only ultimately to the listener who is almost lost in the snow where he is said to listen. The effectual abolition of that listener to a vanishing-point ("nothing himself") makes the poem approach the hiding-places of unintelligibility. But this very hermeticism enables the listener to become, in a Moebius-like turning inside-out, a beholder again (as he had been a regarder and beholder at the beginning). He becomes the Emersonian transparent eyeball not on a bare common but in the midst of an unfamiliar plenitude (snow and ice for the eye, wind for the ear) that he does not want. "Exile desire for what is not," he says in effect to himself: and the receding planes suddenly become entirely frontal again, as he beholds, squarely in front of him, "nothing that is not there and the nothing that is." Without the receding into inaccessibility and remoteness that it manifests, Stevens' diction could not recover itself in such a magisterial reversal of perception. We are drawn by all of Stevens' syntactic involutions into the vertiginous abyss of things thought too long; when they can be no longer thought, then the mind collapses on itself, turns inside-out, and hears the cricket of summer forming itself out of ice. Stevens' bold stroke of the three "nothing's" closing *The Snow Man* announces, as with a closing of one door and the opening of another, the discovery of the abolition of one old self by a new one, which necessitates at first the contemplation of an absolute void. From this discovery comes, eventually, Stevens' great poem of the void, *The Auroras of Autumn*. But we see in *The Snow Man*, through its vertigo of receding planes, the very moment in which Stevens first discovered that the self, pursued to invisibility, makes itself metaphysically visible again, if only in the form of a terrifying blank.

In alluding to a predecessor, Stevens follows the modernist strategy we are familiar with in painting—to take a known content (let us say the *Demoiselles d'Avignon*) and re-do it with violently

altered lines and colors. Stevens in fact explicitly takes up the paint-
ers' strategy in *The Paltry Nude Starts on a Spring Voyage,* where
Botticelli's *Birth of Venus* is the point of reference by which we define
our own modern American Venus, born of a culture lacking
mythology:

> But not on a shell, she starts,
> Archaic, for the sea.
> But on the first-found weed
> She scuds the glitters. . . .
>
> She too is discontent
> And would have purple stuff upon her arms.

Stevens' secrecies of allusion were learned perhaps from Keats; one
reason that Keats's allusions are by no means fully annotated even yet,
is that he rarely announces them; rather, he casually models his own
writing on what he has read, in a form of what Marianne Moore
would call "emotional shorthand." As we learn more about Stevens'
reading, and recognize more of his allusions, many poems will be
clarified, if not necessarily in their substance (we all have read *The
Snow Man* without thinking of Keats) yet certainly in their manner
of becoming, their conduct of themselves.[3]

The next form of secrecy I want to consider is the secrecy of the
implied narrative, and here I turn to another great poem, *The Emper-
or of Ice Cream.* For purposes of experiment, I have put the details
the poem gives us into the form of a first-person narrative; I see the
poem as a rewritten form of this *ur*-narrative, in which the narrative
has been changed into an impersonal form, and the linear temporal
structure of narrative form has been replaced by a strict geometric
spatial construction—two rooms juxtaposed. Here (with apologies)
is my conjectural narrative *ur*-form of the poem, constructed purely
as an explanatory device:

> I went, as a neighbor, to a house to help to lay out the corpse of an
> old woman who had died alone; I was helping to prepare for the home
> wake. I entered, familiarly, not by the front door but by the kitchen
> door. I was shocked and repelled as I went into the kitchen by the
> disorderly festival going on inside: a big muscular neighbor who
> worked at the cigar-factory had been called in to crank the ice-cream
> machine, various neighbors had sent over their scullery-girls to help
> out and their yard-boys bearing newspaper-wrapped flowers from
> their yards to decorate the house and the bier: the scullery-girls were
> taking advantage of the occasion to dawdle around the kitchen and

flirt with the yard-boys, and they were all waiting around to have a taste of the ice-cream when it was finished. It all seemed to me crude and boisterous and squalid and unfeeling in the house of the dead—all that appetite, all that concupiscence.

Then I left the sexuality and gluttony of the kitchen and went in to the death in the bedroom. The corpse of the old woman was lying exposed on the bed. My first impulse was to find a sheet to cover the corpse; I went to the cheap old pine dresser, but it was hard to get the sheet out of it because each of the three drawers was lacking a drawer-pull; she must have been too infirm to get to the store to get new glass knobs. But I got a sheet out, noticing that she had hand-embroidered a fantail border on it; she wanted to make it beautiful, even though she was so poor that she made her own sheets, and cut them as minimally as she could so as to get as many as possible out of a length of cloth. She cut them so short, in fact, that when I pulled the sheet up far enough to cover her face, it was too short to cover her feet. It was almost worse to have to look at her old calloused feet than to look at her face; somehow her feet were more dead, more mute, than her face had been.

She is dead, and the fact cannot be hidden by any sheet. What remains after death, in the cold light of reality, is life—all of that life, with its coarse muscularity and crude hunger and greedy concupiscence, that is going on in the kitchen. The only god of this world is the cold god of persistent life and appetite; and I must look steadily at this repellent but true tableau—the animal life in the kitchen, the corpse in the back bedroom. Life offers no other tableau of reality, once we pierce beneath appearances.

Stevens' secrecy here, as elsewhere, is the secrecy of impersonal address. When he writes the poem, it is as though the voice of Necessity itself is speaking an immortal theater-direction, a naturalistic "Fiat": "Call the roller of big cigars, let the wenches dawdle, let the boys bring flowers, take a sheet, spread it, let the lamp shine." And this is followed by an equally impersonal commentary: "The only emperor is the emperor of ice-cream." Here is the poem:

> Call the roller of big cigars,
> The muscular one, and bid him whip
> In kitchen cups concupiscent curds.
> Let the wenches dawdle in such dress
> As they are used to wear, and let the boys
> Bring flowers in last month's newspapers.
> Let be be finale of seem.
> The only emperor is the emperor of ice-cream.
>
> Take from the dresser of deal,

> Lacking the three glass knobs, that sheet
> On which she embroidered fantails once
> And spread it so as to cover her face.
> If her horny feet protrude, they come
> To show how cold she is, and dumb.
> Let the lamp affix its beam.
> The only emperor is the emperor of ice-cream.

To my mind, this has something of Joyce's "scrupulous meanness." The chill conveyed by the impersonal account conveys, better than any first-person expression of shock and pity and acknowledgment, the absolute necessity of the shock, and the pity, and the final unwilling acknowledgment of a harsh truth. We have, says Stevens' two-stanza spatial structure, no choice in the matter: death and life coexist, side by side. We are shocked by the coarseness of this, and repelled by both the gross physicality of death and the animal greed of life. But in view of the inflexible order of this coexistence, mere "personal reaction" is not an adequate vehicle. The anguish of the poem is the anguish before the absolute predictability of emotion as well as the predictability of situation. The pitiless lamp affixing its beam, the finale of "seem" in "be," the single emperor—everything here is determined, without an inch of personal leeway. The deliberate materiality of the poem, extending equally to concupiscent curds and horny feet, denies the very spontaneity—of personal desire, imagination, romantic love, and poetic vision—which any first-person account of either desire or mourning, by its very nature, implies, and which conventional elegy invokes. Stevens preserves in this poem the conventions of elegy: the corpse, the shroud, the flowers, the mourners, the ceremony of the feast, the mention of inexorable fate, the supreme Minos or Rhadamanthus, the persistence of life in the face of death. But the singing "I" of elegy is ruthlessly suppressed, and with him go at once both the dirge and the apotheosis proper to classical elegy. We may see in this poem a savage refutation of Poe's claim that the death of a beautiful woman is the proper subject for poetry: once again, a classical topic is scrawled violently over with the graffiti of modernism.

Form in Stevens, including the secrecies of form, is always a carrier of meaning. Stevens' obliquities and silent juxtapositions are neither capricious nor dispensable. But until we see what they hide (in the case of the *Emperor*, the prior narrative), we cannot see what they illuminate. In this case, the geometric form illustrates the absolute necessity of choosing between the two rooms. There is no place else to go; you can either be cold and dumb, or you have to join the low concupiscence in the kitchen—and such a "choice" is really no choice at all, so the only emperor is the emperor of ice cream. Stevens' poetry is a poetry of feeling pressed to an extreme; the pressure itself produces the compression and condensation of the work. The pressure of the imagination pressing back against reality, as Stevens called it, is very great: If you confine Greece, Keats, and Tennessee in the same chamber of your mind for a time, the amalgam solidifies into the famous stoneware jar and its preposterous sulky stanzas—"Tell me, what form can possibly suit the slovenly wilderness?" Or if you confine in your mind Keats, the English winter, the New England winter, Shelley's *terza rima* in the *West Wind*, and a wish to reproduce the paradox of beholding a void replete with unintelligible meaning, the elements freeze into an unrhymed *terza rima* poem surrounding the absent figure of the New England Snow Man, our false Florimel unable to conceive of melting, he has been cold for such a long time. And if you confine all those elements from life and literature in a single mind for seventy-five years, the amalgam becomes more and more reduced to those elements, those "few things / For which a fresh name always occurred" (*Local Objects*).

It is to the secrecies of those powerful single images that I now turn, Stevens' secrecy of symbol. Stevens is often called a symbolist poet, and the difficulty of reading him is consequently ascribed to his use of "symbols." The "decoding" of these "symbols" was the first task undertaken by the early critics of Stevens, a decoding in the easy form of equivalence: the sun "was" reality, the moon "was" imagination, green "was" the fertile earth, blue "was" the azure of the creating mind. This decoding produced some commentary of extraordinary banality, in which poem after poem was said to be "about" the encounter between "the imagination" and "reality." Commentary which impoverishes poems is a disservice to them. I think we can see now that for Stevens there was no reality except as we imagine it afresh each day. We see the *Ding-an-sich* every day; it is not hidden from us; but we can only see it *as* we locally see it, in the manner in which we see it today. Appearance, for Stevens, *is* reality. Therefore there is no encounter between "Appearance" and "Reality"—there are only the fresh "realities"—which we may equally call "appearances"—of every day. The expression of newness requires, each day, a new description, which will draw its terms from something in the world. After a while, one has used a number of terms for one's descriptions, and one begins to notice that the terms have established a network among themselves, a referentiality that does not so much extend outward to some putative "real world" as horizontally to the inwardly-extensive world of terms or images.[4] "Thinking of a Relation between the Images of Metaphors" (as Stevens called it) is what all of Stevens' poems do. To see the rich nature of these poems, one must not monotonously refer them to some single external theme, whether physical or metaphysical; rather one must reveal their depth and breadth of internal reference—a reference so full in the last poems as to make them readable only in the light of the earlier poetic illusions to which they allude. To illustrate Stevens' chief form of symbolic secrecy—his self-reference—I want to look at a poem called *The Dove in the Belly*— one of a series of poems about doves (and pigeons, their domestic counterpart) in Stevens.

I have written in my first chapter about Stevens' poem of sexual loneliness in old age, *The Dove in Spring,* and the first poem of secrecy I will take up in this essay is about the same dove. Stevens' secrecy here is both a secrecy of reference and a secrecy of reduction—both techniques are common in his poems. The dove is Venus' dove, though not called here by its mythological name; instead, it is biologically identified as "the dove in the belly." Stevens first alluded to this dove in *Depression before Spring,* when the dawn announced by the crowing of the cock brings no green queen for the abandoned poet: "Ki-ki-ri-ki / Brings no rou-cou, / No rou-cou-cou." The dove appears again in Stevens' violent prayer, in *Ghosts as Cocoons,* to be born again into love; he asks that the ghost of an old murdered love become the cocoon of a new love, a new Psyche to his Cupid; he talks of the dove-winged blendings of the moon, hoping they will bring him a bride and blot out the "mangled smutted semi-world hacked out of dirt." Stevens' bitterest comments on change arise from these disappointments in romantic love, which remained for him the type of all illusion:

Like a rose rabbi, later, I pursued,
And still pursue, the origin and course
Of love.
(*Le Monocle de Mon Oncle,* XII)

Love (as we know from the early poems) promised so much, made
the world so fair with its dove-winged blendings; it combined tempestuous feeling with paradisal peace ("the incredible calm in ec-
stasy"), and it built a nest of solacing music in the heart. Even (as in
The Dove in Spring) when its cooing turns in old age to a small
howling of loss, Stevens is unwilling to let the dove die. And just as
sexual love brings out his most violent language of disillusion, so, in
The Dove in the Belly, when he recalls its transcendent power to
transform the world, it evokes from him his most heartfelt language
of praise. Under the aegis of Venus' dove, he says, the whole world
takes on a glow, an excellence, a beauty, a magical brilliance, and a
fruitfulness that he can never forget; and we ourselves, he continues,
poor and ruined as we are, put on, under the enchantment of the
tempestuous dove hidden in the belly, costumes that make us regal
and ceremonious, like nobles disposed on terraces. Stevens cannot
forbear to hail this miraculous radiance of love, itself a health and a
salvation, inspiring as the dove of the spirit.

The poem begins by seeing all appearance as a contantly-
changing play—as if appearance were a toy for us, to distract and
amuse us. But we cannot be worldly and skeptical too long in the
presence of love; we become instead its celebrators, glad when the
dove who has built his nest in the belly is placated at last. And yet we
recognize here Stevens' characteristic refusal of the first-person,
whether singular or plural, his wish for an impersonal lyric voice:

The Dove in the Belly

The whole of appearance is a toy. For this,
The dove in the belly builds his nest and coos,

Selah, tempestuous bird. How is it that
The rivers shine and hold their mirrors up,

Like excellence collecting excellence?
How is it that the wooden trees stand up

And live and heap their panniers of green
And hold them round the sultry day? Why should

> These mountains being high be, also, bright,
> Fetched up with snow that never falls to earth?
>
> And this great esplanade of corn, miles wide,
> Is something wished for made effectual
>
> And something more. And the people in costumes,
> Though poor, though raggeder than ruin, have that
>
> Within them right for terraces—oh, brave salut!
> Deep dove, placate you in your hiddenness.

Stevens' sketch of the world in this poem is done with his customary primitive simplicity: there are rivers mirroring the sky, wooden trees that come alive and turn green, bright snow-topped mountains that in summer see no snow fall, and an esplanade of ripened corn: sky, water, vegetation, mountains, and the fruits of the earth. And, inhabiting all this, people, poor and ragged, but for a moment costumed and inwardly made grand. And Stevens' celebratory rhetoric could not be simpler, either; "How is it that this can happen to me; Why should the mountains be beautiful with snow as well as high?" It is the rhetoric of hyperbole—this great esplanade, the brave salut of the people. Like most devotees, Stevens fears the god he worships: "Deep dove," he prays, "placate you in your hiddenness." The dove is here a masculine dove, the Holy Spirit of transcendent inspiration confined, "in the belly," with erotic desire: if unplacated he will rage in that destructive chaos described in *Chaos in Motion and Not in Motion*, Stevens' account of a desire that can no longer imagine any possible mate, "Desire without an object of desire, / All mind and violence and nothing felt." Stevens alternates between the happiness I have just been describing in *The Dove in the Belly*, the pain of *The Dove in Spring*, and the absence of the dove in *Chaos in Motion and Not in Motion*. He wishes, as he often does, that change would stop, that for once he could be "the single man / In whose breast, the dove, alighting, would grow still" (*Thinking of a Relation between the Images of Metaphors*). But each time the dove alights he sings a slightly different song; and though each variation comes close to the unstated theme, the dove can never resemble the dove in perfect Platonic indistinguishability. No appearance is identical to an earlier appearance; no feeling is identical to an earlier feeling; and so the task of poetry for Stevens, never ceases. As he explained in a letter (*L,* 852), the necessary angel is reality; reality offers us, over and over, different facets of itself, soliciting our adjustments to it in those re-shiftings of perception and thought and desire that for Stevens define poesis, imagination, the construction of meaning and value. It cannot be said too often that this is an activity that every human being engages in at every moment. How is it, Stevens asks, that we do not stay the same, that we do not keep our first beliefs and our first self-constructs and our first loves? What makes us change? And what makes the last state of affairs better (or worse) than the first? Or are they all equal?

In one sense, of course, these questions are banalities, at least in the abstract (though in the concrete they are painful enough for each one of us). Stevens' tribute to their banality and commonness appears in the simplicity of his reductions, as in *The Dove in the Belly*. But his tribute to the unique import of the questions as they are lived by each of us appears in his devising of a unique situation and form for each poem. Like life, the poem, he said, must resist the intelligence almost successfully. It must present itself as an enigma, just as life does. We live out each poem as we live inside it. The poem-as-passage, not the poem-as-discourse, is Stevens' model, even when he appears most discursive. Consequently, each of his embodiments of the predicament of illusion or loss or reinstated belief or love is stylized into a nonce event in the shorter poems; and Stevens' commitment to the secrecy of intertextual symbols like the dove, as well as to the secrecies of an impersonal presentation and a resolutely elliptical discourse, makes him a poet knowable in the instance only when he is known in the whole.

We have seen a group of Stevens' secrecies; but I want to close with Stevens' late disavowing of secrecy—or his exploding or implosion of it. All the appeal of secrecy for Stevens arises from the wish not to betray, in both senses of the word, the contrary oscillations of his spirit. He wanted, in *The Snow Man,* to show that he both agreed, and did not agree, with Keats's point about the amnesia of nature, taking Keats as a point of departure and yet departing from him; he wanted, in *The Emperor of Ice Cream,* to acknowledge intellectually the simultaneous cohabiting of concupiscence and corpses without assenting, tonally, to their appalling co-presence; he wanted *The Dove in the Belly* to proclaim the hybridizing of the Holy Spirit with the visceral dove of Venus without appearing either blasphemous or ridiculous; and he wanted, in *Anecdote of the Jar,* to position an American jar on a new continent without forgetting the urns of Greece or the stanzas of England. Finally, however, in each of these endeavors, "a complex of emotions falls apart" (*Credences of Summer*). The sheer effort of finding a medium of verbal solubility for the vocabularies of Romanticism and modernism (as in the meditations on Keats) or for concupiscence and corporeal mortality (as in the *Emperor*), or for the Holy Spirit and Venus (as in *The Dove in the Belly*) seems not only impossible but perhaps deceptive. If there is no medium of verbal solubility, perhaps one can only imagine two immiscible liquids with a metonymic impermeability. Stevens writes, in this mood of wanting to assert immiscibility, a poem almost unreadable, *The Hermitage at the Center.* It is a double-column poem, but written out with the right-hand elements (which describe the eternal fiction of desire achieved in words—Venus surrounded by her doves which make an intelligible twittering) following the left-hand elements (which describe the collapse of freshness of utterance into the twice-told, the incoherent, and the meaningless—falling leaves, a tottering wind, and unintelligible thought). It is only by a great effort of will that Stevens can resume the two columns into one at the end, by reciting one of the oldest of religious gnomic utterances, one he had used earlier in *An Ordinary Evening in New Haven:* "And yet this end and this beginning are one." This fiction of the circular, of a primitive like an orb, informs Stevens' use of Alpha and Omega. He could not see any way that freshness could be purchased except by dissolution; nor could he see any freshness remaining unravaged by skeptical thought and emotional attrition. Here is his dilemma, as he visits his hermitage, his place of central recourse:

> The leaves on the macadam make a noise—
> How soft the grass on which the desired
> Reclines in the temperature of heaven—
>
> Like tales that were told the day before yesterday—
> Sleek in a natural nakedness,
> She attends the tintinnabula—
>
> And the wind sways like a great thing tottering—
> Of birds called up by more than the sun,
> Birds of more wit, that substitute—

> Which suddenly is all dissolved and gone—
> Their intelligible twittering
> For unintelligible thought.
> And yet this end and this beginning are one,
> And one last look at the ducks is a look
> At lucent children round her in a ring.

Stevens wrote this poem about the Elizabeth Park in Hartford, where he took frequent walks. It had a duck pond; and one of his looks at the ducks would be, he knew, his last. It is impossible to count the number of times he had looked at the ducks—each time he looked, he saw them in a new relation. The daily impersonal newness of the visible world was at first a disturbing thought to Stevens, as we know from the phenomenology, both visual and affective, of *Sea-Surface Full of Clouds;* it made for a troubling relativity of value (any scene is as valuable as any other scene, any mood is as true as any other mood). But now, at the end of his life, that aesthetic inexhaustibility of the world and the emotions is Stevens' only principle of faith: after every Omega an Alpha is sure to follow, and one last look at the ducks is a look at lucent children, making one more perfect orb, phrased in the childishness of a budding aesthetic—the children are "round her in a ring."

This last Venus is not only erotic but maternal (stripped of her maternal sinister possibilities exposed in *Madame La Fleurie);* the intelligible twittering of her birds stands in the aesthetic order for what her children stand for in the order of nature—a harmonious replication of self guaranteeing the persistence of identity. In the hermitage at the center lives the poet, scholar-hermit, snow man, in his desolate landscape of leaves and miserable wind; but in the center there also lives the interior paramour, the fictive reclining nude amid her doves (here turned to ducks) and children. Being there together, as the Muse says in the *Final Soliloquy,* is "enough." But this last poem cannot patch the world quite round, even with its closing fiction of the merging of the left-hand and right-hand columns of the poem into one. It abandons the secrecy of concealed tensions for an open revelation of the chasm between the world of misery and the world of desire. It exposes secrecy for what it is—another fiction.

Stevens' secrecies have claims on us only because they are, in the end, not mystifications; and because he knew their living components and their veiled hostilities; and because the fiction they represent, that of a verbal medium in which all oppositions could coexist, is one without which poetry could not be written.

4. PERFECTION
"Washed away by magnitude"

The topic I want to take up in this final chapter is the topic of magnitude. When I first read *The Comedian as the Letter C*, I heard an echo that I could not place in the line, "Crispin was washed away by magnitude." It was only later that I recognized its parent-line in Keats's sonnet on the Elgin marbles, works of art which seemed to Keats "a shadow of a magnitude." Crispin was washed away by the magnitude of the ocean, by its one, vast, subjugating, final tone. Crispin, of course, re-establishes himself; but for Stevens the struggle of the artifact with external magnitude was renewed very often, frequently taking the form of the relation between poet-protagonist and ocean, as in the examples I quote.

I choose magnitude for my rubric because it seems to avoid, as a category, that scheme or dialectical opposition so often invoked in books and essays on Stevens. Our sense of Stevens' antinomies has perhaps led us into a reduction of his poetry into "the imagined and the real, thought / And the truth, Dichtung and Wahrheit." These antitheses are then seen to lead inexorably to a synthesis. (In *The Man with the Blue Guitar*, from which I have been quoting, the synthesis may follow immediately, as in "All confusion solved," or it may appear as a copulative solution of opposites, "Oxidia is Olympia.") These rhetorical postures in Stevens have led to critical declarations which first expose the contrary theses and then triumphantly, following the poems, expose the synthesis, making Stevens into his own Canon Aspirin:

He had to choose. But it was not a choice
Between excluding things. It was not a choice
Between, but of. He chose to include the things
That in each other are included, the whole,
The complicate, the amassing harmony.
     (*Notes toward a Supreme Fiction,* "It Must Give Pleasure," VI)

61

These final syntheses are consoling ones, and yet Stevens himself wished not to console or sanctify, but plainly to propound. The dialectical model for consideration of his poetry, in which a recognition of anthitheses, however full, usually yields to a diapason of synthesis, seems to me oddly at variance with the taste of much of the poetry on the tongue, a taste at once more astringent and more provisional than that offered by either antitheses or synthesis. It is in the hope of finding a problematic less foreordained in its dimensions than the dialectical one (since, as Stevens said, "Progress in any aspect is a movement through changes in terminology" [*OP*, 157]), that I turn to the question of magnitude and the problems it set for Stevens, restricting myself, although unnaturally for this topic, to the limits of the short poems.

The first question, a historical one which Stevens inherited, is to decide the locus of magnitude. Decisively rejecting the celestial locus, Wordsworth had asked whether it is in man that we find magnitude, or in nature. *The Comedian as the Letter C,* inheriting that question, begins Stevens' career with a nod in the direction of nature. But the early poem *For an Old Woman in a Wig* rebukes man's interest in "the sweeping / Poetry of sky and sea," his fondness for "the circumference of earth's impounding," and recommends instead that he seek out "the unknown new" in his "surrounding," thereby anticipating *The Man on the Dump.*

Stevens quotes *Hamlet* in *For an Old Woman,* and shares Hamlet's contrary views of man; that he is a fellow crawling between earth and heaven or, conversely, that he is a masterwork angelic or even godlike. In Stevens' comic moments, as he contemplates man placed between earth and heaven, he can say (through Broomstick in this instance), "There's no truer comedy than this hodge-podge of men and sunlight, women and moonlight, houses and clouds, and so on" (*Bowl, Cat, and Broomstick*). This difference in magnitude between the single mind and the limitless universe it contemplates is Stevens' earliest problem of magnitude. One of his first responses to the disproportion of what he would later represent as the single candle of the mind fearful of the powerful auroras stretching across the heavens is simply to deny any disproportion, and find a perfectly congruent relation—an exquisite fitting, we might call it from Wordsworth—of the mind to the external world. In *Bowl, Cat, and*

Broomstick, Bowl speaks, translating the poem of a twenty-two year old poetess:

> In the movement of trees, I find my own agitation . . . . The forms of trees are the only images in my mind.

Bowl explicates:

> She means that the images in her mind are of the forms of trees and that there are no other images there.

In spite of various subsequent ironies—the poetess turns out to be not twenty-two but forty-six, and her poems are mocked—we know that the poetess' conviction of the interpenetration of mind and nature was Stevens' own. Stevens even tried the posture of denying any difference in magnitude between body, mind, garments, environment, and nature, as we can see in the involutions of *Infanta Marina,* a poem about a seaside "creature of the evening":

> Her terrace was the sand
> And the palms and the twilight.
>
> She made of the motions of her wrist
> The grandiose gestures
> Of her thought.
>
> The rumpling of the plumes
> Of this creature of the evening
> Came to be sleights of sails
> Over the sea.
>
> And thus she roamed
> In the roamings of her fan,
>
> Partaking of the sea,
> And of the evening,
> As they flowed around
> And uttered their subsiding sound.

Each of the five stanzas (three preliminary and two conclusive) of the poem is a statement of relation: in the first, the *sand* and the *palms* and the *twilight* (representing earth, vegetation, and air) are said to be the Infanta's terrace, her architectural setting; in the second, she is said to make the grandiose gestures of her *thought* out of the bodily motions of her *wrist;* in the third, the *rumpling of her plumes* came to be *sleights of sails* over the sea; in the fourth, *she* is said to roam in the roamings of her *fan;* and in the fifth *she* is said to partake of the *sea* and the *evening,* "as they flowed around / And uttered their subsiding sound." It is only with hindsight, perhaps, that we see certain problems concealed, even suppressed, in the calm progress of this poem. The greatest problem is that sound (as in *The Snow Man* and many later poems, notably *Not Ideas about the Thing But the Thing Itself* and *The Course of a Particular*) is here predicated only of nature (in this poem seen as the sea and the evening, elsewhere as the wind or the leaves) and not of man; the Infanta can make wrist motions, can rumple her plumes and follow the roamings of her fan, can even make the grandiose gestures of her thought, but utterance is beyond her. The corrective to the Infanta will be the girl in *The Idea of Order at Key West,* who is endowed with the power to sing (with consequent different problems, to which I will come). But for the moment, to return to the Infanta, it appears that this seaside princess (called a Spanish "infanta" because she is speechless—*infans*—and because we are in that Florida which is the Spanish *tierra florida*) gains her untroubled relation with her surroundings only by forgoing language, by remaining mute. Stevens' verbs of relation here are deliberately varied: after the simple copula of possession we see first her agency *making* thought of motion; next the movements of her accoutrements *coming to be* movements of sails; thirdly herself *moving in the movements* of one accoutrement; and finally *partaking of* nature. The sense in which things belong to her and she belongs to other things shifts constantly; in "her terrace was the sand," the terrace is not hers as her wrist is, or her thought is, or her fan is. In one sense the whole poem is a double scherzo on "her" in the possessive sense, and on "of," punned on in its partitive and possessive senses:

> of the motions
> of her wrist
> of her thought
> of the plumes
> of this creature
> of the evening
> of sails
> of her fan
> of the sea
> of the evening

The litany of "of's" states syntactically what the poem states semantically—that everything can be part of everything else on an equal basis. To say that motions and wrist and thought and plumes and creature and evening and sails and fan and sea and evening can all, in fifteen short lines, be objects of the preposition "of" is to say that they can all fill the same slot, which is to say be identified with, and substitutable for, each other. In short, there is no difference in order of magnitude or significance among them.

Five years earlier, in 1916, Stevens had published a poem called *Domination of Black*, which he selected much later—in 1942—as his best poem for an anthology called *This Is My Best*,[1] thereby marking a quarter-century's approbation of the poem.

Domination of Black

At night, by the fire,
The colors of the bushes
And of the fallen leaves,
Repeating themselves,
Turned in the room,
Like the leaves themselves
Turning in the wind.
Yes: but the color of the heavy hemlocks
Came striding.
And I remembered the cry of the peacocks.

The colors of their tails
Were like the leaves themselves
Turning in the wind,
In the twilight wind.
They swept over the room,
Just as they flew from the boughs of the hemlocks
Down to the ground.
I heard them cry—the peacocks.
Was it a cry against the twilight
Or against the leaves themselves
Turning in the wind,
Turning as the flames
Turned in the fire,
Turning as the tails of the peacocks
Turned in the loud fire,
Loud as the hemlocks
Full of the cry of the peacocks?
Or was it a cry against the hemlocks?

Out of the window,
I saw how the planets gathered
Like the leaves themselves
Turning in the wind.

I saw how the night came,
Came striding like the color of the heavy hemlocks.
I felt afraid.
And I remembered the cry of the peacocks.

This poem affirms dramatically an absolute order of magnitude in which night (Stevens' figure for death) dominates despotically over every other order of magnitude, including nature, utterance, and mind itself. In this complicated poem, utterance is either part of meaninglessness or an outcry against it, but the distinction is itself meaningless since night quenches all utterance. A disorienting disproportion of elements prevails; we last see the speaker in terror at the gathering of planets and the oncoming night "striding like the color of the heavy hemlocks." He beholds a magnitude against which he is powerless; unlike Crispin he will not, it seems, be made new by this immersion in magnitude. These poems I have quoted suffice to show that Stevens' perception of magnitude changes form very often; and often, as in *Infanta Marina*, he denies orders of magnitude altogether. The aesthetic problem for Stevens in this respect is threefold: where to locate magnitude, if it exists; how to express magnitude, if it exists; and how to deny magnitude, if in fact, in spite of appearances, it does not exist.

Stevens is careful, I believe, to represent different orders of magnitude by different vocabularies and structures; if he wishes to assert that man and nature are of comparable orders of magnitude, as in *Infanta Marina*, he is bound to use parallel structures. *Domination of Black*, on the other hand, is a scherzo on *different* prepositions and conjunctions (while *Infanta Marina* was a scherzo on the *one* preposition "of"). *Domination of Black* shows all possible relations (whether a relation by "of" or by "in" or by "like" or by "over" or by "from" or by "to" or by "against" or by "as") as equally impotent against the night. The various living or moving orders of being—colors, vegetative nature (leaves), animal nature (the peacocks), natural motion (the wind), household life (the hearth-fire), cosmic life (the planets), and natural utterance (the cry of the peacocks)—are all assimilated to each other by the sinuous prepositions and conjunctions of the poem until they become indistinguishable; against all these orders of being is set another color (black), another natural reality (night), another vegetation (the Stygian hemlocks), and by implication, another order of being—death, perhaps suicide. Of course, the despotic order of magnitude asserted dramatically by the repetitive weight placed on night, black, and the hemlocks is countered by the pride of place given to the peacocks and their ambiguous cry; they are the climax of each of the three stanzas. A presentational magnitude of location in the case of the peacocks, then, is opposed to a dramatic magnitude of assertion of blackness, and we might say that animal utterance and meaninglessness come to a standoff. The poem allows itself certain permissions: animal utterance can take place naturally in the cry of the peacocks; and it can be assimilated as the most intimate possession of the human speaker; no metaphysical discontinuity mars his easy incorporation of the peacock's cry. To that extent, the poem is not one of "difficultest rigor"; we must look forward for that to the great poem *Of Mere Being* (which we might re-name *Domination of Gold),* from which Holly Stevens rightly drew the title for her edition of the poems. There, in the palm at the end of the mind, a golden bird in a bronze decor sings "without human meaning, without human feeling." Stevens' denial there of the pathetic fallacy is a retraction of the way in which *Domination of Black* places its peacock-cry; that cry appears so squarely and climactically in the poem that human feeling must be ascribed to it, since the speaker claims it, as a last resort, as a magnitude to oppose to the magnitude of night.

Both of the early poems I have quoted, *Infanta Marina* and *Domination of Black,* owe a good deal to the Chinoiserie of Pound and Amy Lowell, but the poems also contain elements of the later Stevens; we find in *Domination of Black* that gathering of the planets which will be repeated later in *The Auroras of Autmn;* and we find in *Infanta Marina* those sleights of sails whose elements reappear in many poems, from *The Sense of the Sleight-of-Hand Man* to *The Sail of Ulysses.* Planets and sailboats are both Stevensian, though belonging to very different orders of magnitude. Stevens links, or attempts to link, the orders of magnitude they represent in *The Idea of Order at Key West.* The linking mechanism here between sailboats and planets is a female walker by the shore, an older or more developed *Infanta Marina,* one who has learned to sing. It is significant that the poem is no longer named after its female figure, in the way that the earlier poem was named after the Infanta or as another was named after the Paltry Nude. Instead, this poem has a conceptual name (*The Idea of Order*); Stevens will continue to vacillate all his life between titles derived from a personal protagonist and titles derived from a proposition. In *The Idea of Order* the two Wordsworthian orders of mind and world, which were so easily interpenetrative in *Infanta Marina*, seem to be at the same time exquisitely fitted and yet subtly uneasy with each other: the girl, Stevens concedes, may indeed utter in her song what she hears in the song of the sea, but now, with the introduction of the problem of language, the discrepancy between the two cries, inhuman and human, strikes the poet far more than any similarity:

> The song and the water were not medleyed sound
> Even if what she sang was what she heard,
> Since what she sang was uttered word by word.
> It may be that in all her phrases stirred
> The grinding water and the gasping wind;
> But it was she and not the sea we heard.

This announcement of discontinuity between two orders, the voice of nature and the voice of the singer,[2] does not in itself establish any difference in magnitude between the two orders. Stevens decides, or appears to decide, that the human voice, given its powerful effects, is of a greater order of magnitude than the voice of the ocean; he consequently must decide how to represent the greater magnitude of the singer's power. He resorts here to his most common early device for the distinction of orders of magnitude, the comparative and superlative degree:

> It was *more* than that.
> *More* even than her voice, and ours, among
> The meaningless plungings of water and the wind . . . .
> It was her voice that made
> The sky *acutest* at its vanishing. [my italics]

It is no accident, either, that the singer is represented by the verb that represented the domination of black; just as the night came "striding," so her listeners "beheld her striding there alone." But two more insistings on the superior order of magnitude of the singer's song follow, betraying Stevens' uneasiness with his own establishing of difference in those orders. First of all, the power of the singer's song is transferred by its hearers, as a new energy, to the lights of the fishing boats which take on a geographical and magical power over nature, as they master the night, portion out the sea, fix emblazoned zones and fiery poles (as geographers do by their systems of latitude and longitude), and arrange, deepen, and enchant night. This geographical and emotional mastery in the lights, the projected effect of hearing the song, is followed, secondly, by the hymn to the blessed rage to order words in—and here the comparative recurs—"*ghostlier* demarcations, *keener* sounds." There is an uneasiness which persists, however, even in this confident hymn. Stevens' relative crudeness of representation here is visible in his use of the comparative, the superlative, and various insistent verbs of mastering, apportioning, fixing, arranging, deepening, and evaluating; it is visible as well in the final revealing, if truthful, ascription of rage to the maker and ghostliness to the results. Stevens' powers of representation are being strained, in praising here the order of putatively superior magnitude, in asserting the power of poetry over nature. The order of lesser magnitude, the sea and its cry, are on the whole described with less strain. I will not stop on the very interesting details of that description, but only recall the ghostliness and pathos of the "body wholly body, fluttering its empty sleeves," that "ever-hooded, tragic-gestured sea," that landscape of "theatrical distances, bronze shadows heaped / On high horizons, mountainous atmospheres / Of sky and sea."

When Stevens later "rewrote" or "reimagined" *The Idea of Order at Key West*, he called it by the occluded name *Somnambulisma*,[3] which I take to mean thoughts thought (or things said) while sleepwalking, truer perhaps (like Lady Macbeth's utterances) than what the waking self might allow, but still not allowed the ontological status of ideas about the thing. The poem *Somnambulisma*, a "wakefulness inside a sleep" (*Long and Sluggish Lines*), takes its origin from the line I quoted when I began, "Crispin was washed away by magnitude." Here, remembering the *Ode to a Nightingale* and Keats's exemption of the bird from the tragic rhythm of hungry generations, Stevens creates his own corrective mortal Crispin-bird, which resembles in its restlessness the restlessness of the ocean. Yet the ocean continually effaces the bird and its progeny:

On an old shore, the vulgar ocean rolls
Noiselessly, noiselessly, resembling a thin bird,
That thinks of settling, yet never settles, on a nest.

The wings keep spreading and yet are never wings.
The claws keep scratching on the shale, the shallow shale,
The sounding shallow, until by water washed away.

The generations of the bird are all
By water washed away. They follow after.
They follow, follow, follow, in water washed away.

And hollow, hollow, hollow, all delight," we answer to Stevens' Tennysonian onomatopoeia. The difference here from *The Idea of Order*—with its confident talk of mastery and striding and making worlds and ordering words—is striking. The bird, Stevens' first of two figures substituted for the singer, is the attenuated genius of the shore—thin, homeless, abortive, unformed, poor, defeated, its generations as ephemeral, if as persistent, as itself. The vulgar ocean (itself the originating double of the bird) alone seems strong. But Stevens turns, and makes an affirmation comparable to the one which, in *The Idea of Order,* "established" the superior magnitude of the singer's song over the cry of the ocean. To my mind, he here finds a truer representation of a superior order, declaring that were it not for the bird and its generations the ocean would be "a geography of the dead," not a Hades but a desolate nature; it would seem uninhabited because it would have been unsung, unanalyzed, by those who have died.

The second figure here substituted for the singer at Key West is the scholar (in this respect the poem fails, I think, to cohere, since it needs two figures, the bird and the scholar, as a composite to represent the poet). Nonetheless, the invention of the scholar is a fine effort; it incorporates a prizing of that truth and knowledge which a bird alone, as Keats discovered, could not incarnate ("O fret not after knowledge," said the thrush, "I have none"):

Without this bird that never settles, without
Its generations that follow in their universe,
The ocean, falling and falling on the hollow shore,

Would be a geography of the dead; not of that land
To which they may have gone, but of the place in which
They lived, in which they lacked a pervasive being,

In which no scholar, separately dwelling,
Poured forth the fine fins, the gawky beaks, the personalia,
Which, as a man feeling everything, were his.

The endangering sentimentality of *The Idea of Order* lies in the girl's becoming entirely the maker of the world she sings. Here the scholar—Stevens' scholar of one candle—dwells separately, "in a moving solitude" (*OP*, 243) in but not of the world. He redeems the world from death ("Poetry," as Stevens said, "is a means of redemption" [*OP*, 160]), not by arranging or mastering or enchanting, but literally by vivifying, generating true life, a pervasive being, in an otherwise dead world. ("Life," as one of the *Adagia* says, "is not people and scene but thought and feeling" [*OP*, 170].) The representation of the scholar's superiority to the order of nature is anti-Wordsworthian, in that for Stevens nature alone, however restless, is lifeless until the scholar pours forth a population to fill it. In a metaphor borrowed from Genesis, from the day when God created fishes, beasts, and birds, the scholar is said to "pour forth" (like Keats's nightingale) "the fine fins, the gawky beaks, the personalia, / which, as a man feeling everything, were his." The source of creation are sometimes fine (their fineness and their finniness almost one), sometimes gawky, like a newborn bird, but always alive. The singer at Key West had been a maker and a master, regal in her creation and possession of the world; but this scholar, who depends, since "poetry is the scholar's art" (*OP*, 167), on the restless bird, the singing voice within him, "pours forth" (the verb allies him also to the ocean) not regalia but personalia; he is no king in the universe but only another person in the mass, singularly talented but not different, except in that talent, from his fellows. In admitting the meagerness of the bird's life and activity, and the awkwardness and ordinariness of the scholar's productions, Stevens has moved from the easy hyperbole of *The Idea of Order* to a more modest truth—without, however, sacrificing the wish to assert a superior order of magnitude. This strategy of magnitude still continues the use of analogy with the God of Genesis which was present in the world-making activities of the girl at Key West, but the strategy changes as Stevens invents the hypothesis of a birdless world, a geography of the dead, (only hinted at in the empty sleeves in the earlier poem) and finally depends on the single superlative of feeling—feeling "everything"—in the final line.

However, Stevens had suspected, as early as *Harmonium*, that there may be no orders of magnitude at all. The hissing bantam of the personal is as ridiculous as the strutting cock of the universal; the ordinary women rise from the poverty of dry catarrhs, and flit to guitars, only to discover the poverty of dry guitars and flit back to catarrhs. *The Ordinary Women* is remarkable for its mordant satire of the appeal of guitars; in it, all the things that other poems hold sacred—night, moonlight, palaces, garments, alphabets, music, illuminations, sanctity, marriage, beaches, coiffures, fans, desire, and "puissant speech"—are made faintly or overtly repellent. Since Stevens believed that the final poem would be "the poem of fact in the language of fact" (*OP*, 164) the revulsion betrayed by *The Ordinary Women* at the fact that music is of no greater magnitude than nature cannot be allowed to prevail. Nor can the idea expressed in *Gubbinal* that the order of nature (in this case, the sun) is of a different magnitude from the sad and ugly order of society. If all these orders are simply co-present and equal, then a way must be found for that fact to present itself as fact, without revulsion or special pleading. *The Snow Man* makes a brave beginning in this direction, but Stevens cannot write the true poem of equilibrated fact, without resentment, giving each equal order of magnitude its due, until the end of his life.

Stevens' last variation on the central *topos* of *Infanta Marina* and *The Idea of Order* and *Somnambulisma*—that *topos* of someone standing by moving water interpreting it—equalizes the various orders of magnitude by the self-extinction of the singer-scholar-bird. The poem, named not for a protagonist (like *Infanta Marina*), not for a concept (like *The Idea of Order*), not for a less-than-conceptual dream (like *Somnambulisma*), but at last for the thing itself, is the great hymn *The River of Rivers in Connecticut*.

> There is a great river this side of Stygia,
> Before one comes to the first black cataracts
> And trees that lack the intelligence of trees.
>
> In that river, far this side of Stygia,
> The mere flowing of the water is a gayety,
> Flashing and flashing in the sun. On its banks,
>
> No shadow walks. The river is fateful,
> Like the last one. But there is no ferryman.
> He could not bend against its propelling force.
>
> It is not to be seen beneath the appearances
> That tell of it. The steeple at Farmington
> Stands glistening and Haddam shines and sways.

It is the third commonness with light and air,
A curriculum, a vigor, a local abstraction . . .
Call it, once more, a river, an unnamed flowing,

Space-filled, reflecting the seasons, the folk-lore
Of each of the senses; call it, again and again,
The river that flows nowhere, like a sea.

The title announces by its use of the formula "X of X's"—Holy of
Holies, King of Kings—the apparently transcendent order of magnitude of the river, but that order, as we shall see, is finally of no more
significance than any other order. The line on which the whole poem
turns is the line abolishing the Infanta, the Singer, and the Scholar all
at once: "On its banks, / No shadow walks." Nor is there a striding
or dominating figure, here represented (in negation) by a sailor; not
even Charon, the only sailor who can navigate the Styx, dominates
this water: "There is no ferryman. He could not bend against its
propelling force." Since in poetry to mention a presence, even to deny
its existence, is to confer at least a reminiscent existence upon it, we
find the hitherto dominating presence of the inhabitant-princess-
singer-navigator-scholar recalled but declared unnecessary. The rhetorical mode of the poem is that of oral folk-tale, with folk-lore's
immemorial authority over questions of this world and other worlds:
"There is a great river this side of Stygia . . . ." The narrator, we
conclude, has been to Stygia, on the further shore of the Styx: the
river of rivers in Connecticut, he says as one who has traveled, lies on
this side of the fateful Styx, before one comes to the Stygian landscape of "black cataracts / And trees that lack the intelligence of
trees." The narrator is a revenant; to put it more factually, this is the
poem of an old man who has been, as we say, to death's door and
who has been granted a reprieve; as he returns to life he beholds the
stream of life in nature (which he has often scorned as meaningless
and in need of interpretation) and finds it purely good.[4] It no longer
seems pathetic, fluttering empty sleeves; no longer vulgar, rolling on
its hollow shore; no longer eroding, washing men and birds away.
Instead, it is, though fateful, a pure gaiety. The late poem *The River
of Rivers* will not invoke the imagination or the poet's duty to
imagine well, as though imagining were an ethical or practical act.
Rather, "We think, then, as the sun shines or does not"; there is a
"world / Whose blunt laws make an affectation of mind," as Stevens

put it in another late poem, *Looking Across the Fields and Watching the Birds Fly.* This poem is a very late rewriting of *Blanche McCarthy*, an early poem in which Stevens urged himself to look in "the terrible mirror of the sky," rather than in a mirror reflecting the self; in the mirror of the sky one could search "the glare of revelations going by" and see "the wings of stars. / Upward, from unimagined coverts, fly." The apocalyptic and hysterical note of *Blanche McCarthy* has disappeared of course from the late poetry, as has the simpleminded expression of preference for one, putatively superior, order of magnitude, that of nature: "Look in the terrible mirror of the sky / and not in this dead glass" (an exhortation perhaps echoing Yeats—"Beloved, gaze in thine own heart," etc.). *Looking across the Fields* is dated 1952; *The River of Rivers* 1953; the first enunciates the late metaphysics of the toleration of all orders, the second celebrates the concurrence of all orders, both orders of magnitude and orders of relation. These orders include the order of resemblance between worlds ("The river is fateful, / Like the last one"), the order of transcendence of kind ("the river of rivers"), the orders of appearance and reality (the river "is not to be seen beneath the appearances / That tell of it"), the order of the invisible ("light and air"), the order of metaphysics ("a curriculum, a vigor, a local abstraction"), the order of the senses, perceiving the glistening and shining of things, the orders of time (the seasons) and space, and, most centrally for Stevens' mythology, the order represented by the capacious and voluble sea, that washes all away.

It is hard to know how to praise a poem that so expertly sustains before us, in a wonderful equality, all the orders that had jostled for precedence in earlier poems. This is the moment, perhaps, to quote two of Stevens' remarks on form, by which he usually means style:

> Form alone and of itself is an ever-youthful, ever-vital beauty. The principle of music [or we may say poetry, is] humanity itself in other than human form. (*The Whole Man, OP,* 233)

> Manner is something that has not yet been disengaged adequately. It does not mean style; it means the attitude of the writer, his bearing rather than his point of view.
> (*The Irrational Element in Poetry, OP,* 220)

The "subject" of *The River of Rivers in Connecticut* is the inestimable preciousness of the total stream of life as it is seen by one who has had a glimpse of a Stygian darkness beyond, where there await him dark cataracts which can wash all away in an absolute manner not to be compared with life's contingent attritions, and where, if trees lack the intelligence of trees, men will certainly lack the intelligence of men. The poetry of the subject must lie in that contrast between the dark unintelligibility there and the preciousness of life here; the contrast must be drawn, the preciousness made real. The contrast is here ably drawn by being thrice drawn, once in each of the first three tercets. In the first tercet the narrator is so preoccupied with imminent death, so concentrated on Stygia, that he has only the literal denomination "a great river" for his precious life-current, while he has a whole landscape for Stygia. In the second tercet the focus on Stygia has lessened, as the narrator insists that life is still blessedly present, that the river is not only "this side of Stygia" but "far this side of Stygia," and the river takes on pleasure and brilliance:

> The mere flowing of the water is a gayety
> Flashing and flashing in the sun.

In the third tercet, the Styx provides the elemental measure against which any life-river must be defined both by contrast and by comparison:

> On its banks
> No shadow walks. The river is fateful
> Like the last one. But there is no ferryman.
> He could not bend against its propelling force.

At this point, the Styx and its Stygian landscape vanish entirely from the poem, never to return. The mere force of the river seems to have banished them, as "in golden fury" spring "vanishes" (as Stevens said in *Notes,* punning on "vanquish") "the scraps of winter."

With the exorcism of death complete, the poem can begin its second half, where we might expect at once another celebration of the river's force or gaiety. Instead, the river as a concept disappears, and the reasoning mind which conceives of something called "the river of life" recedes in favor of the revived senses; these remark the particulars which the mind conceptualizes only with its later reasoning. The river

> Is not to be seen beneath the appearances
> That tell of it.

The appearances, giving us our only access to the concept, are given their full particularizing by the attribution of their local names; their full impressionist value bathes the grateful senses:

> The steeple at Farmington
> Stands glistening and Haddam shines and sways.

This new-rinsed world is the one seen with the famished eye of the revenant from darkness, who has been able to return from Stygia, at the last moment, to his own familiar steeples and towns in Connecticut, that state whose name, translated from the Indian, is "the place of many rivers." Flowing and flashing belong to the river; glistening and shining and swaying belong to the appearances that tell of it. Light and air, too, move and flash, and Stevens begins his powerful gathering of elements by remembering the epigraph (from Mario Rossi) prefacing his *Evening Without Angels:* "The great interests of man: air and light, the joy of having a body, the voluptuousness of looking." In redefining the elements of this world, Stevens eliminates earth, as too heavy, and fire, as too celestial; his world is composed of water, light, and air.

The joy of having a body, the voluptuousness of looking, are embodied in the river which is the third commonness with light and air. These great interests are, in Stevens' pun, a curriculum, from which we learn; they are a vigor (the flowing and flashing) and a local abstraction (local because they are in Farmington and Haddam, abstract because not to be seen beneath the appearances that tell of them). The summarizing words "the third commonness," "a curriculum, a vigor, a local abstraction" might conclude the poem, were it not that the river is one of the things for which, for Stevens, fresh names always occur; and while he enjoys at present a respite from Stygia, it will not be a long one. Back from Stygia, he is bound to write down his renewed perception of the boundlessness and amplitude of life. "Call it, once more, a river," he adjures himself, and continues without ceasing, "call it, again and again," by name. The two river-names differ. The first names the river by its wonderful motion and its equally wonderful comprehensiveness, mirroring space, nature, time, and the instinctive mythology of the senses:

> Call it, once more, a river, an unnamed flowing,
> Space-filled, reflecting the seasons, the folk-lore
> Of each of the senses.

This Kantian naming suggests,that the categories of time and space
are projected by us onto the river, and seem inseparable from it. The
second naming calls it not "a river" but "the river" and is a darker
specification:

> Call it, again and again,
> The river that flows nowhere, like a sea.

This broadening of the river into something like a sea, everywhere
present, everywhere in motion, but directionless, is Stevens' gentlest
specification of life as meaningless motion, a characterization of life
that had, in poems like *Chaos in Motion and Not in Motion,* pro-
voked some of his harshest lines. This self-adjuration, by an old man
who has glimpsed death, to write more and yet more poems, calling
the unnamed river by more and more names, displays in itself that
fortitude in Stevens admired by Marianne Moore.

But the ease of the poem is more admirable even than its fortitude. Significance and magnitude are here granted to everything—to
the constructs of the senses, to the mind, to the mere motions of the
world, to local appearances, to mighty abstractions, to folk-lore, to
time and space, to gaiety, to solemnity, to observation, to expression,
to fear and to rejoicing, to everywhere, and, literally, to nowhere. In
this Keatsian poem, even Stygian melancholy is necessary as the
contrastive measure by which joy is known. But the Keatsian anguish
of rhetoric, so frequent in early and middle Stevens, does not appear
in this late poem. The magnitudes coexist—but not in the tortured
antitheses of the Weeping Burgher, not in the mannered reciprocities
of *Infanta Marina,* not in the domination of black or the mastery of a
striding singer, not even in the dauntless creativity of the scholar
pouring forth personalia. Here the magnitudes—all of them—simply
are, in a metonymic relation, lying side by side in a fraternity of
shared being.

The form that the poem seems at first to take is that of the old
agon, the vanquishing of the forces of darkness by the forces of light.
By its form, then, it seems to specify two orders of magnitude: one,
the river, victorious and superior; the other, Stygia, defeated and
apparently inferior, since it vanishes after its overshadowing darkness gradually lessens in each of the first three stanzas. Yet in effect,
after presenting both orders, Stevens, in a canceling gesture that may
recall George Herbert, establishes with one word a third order—

nowhere—which dissolves darkness and light alike, and seems to oppose the dualistic folk-lore of the poem (the River of Rivers and Stygia), with yet another dualism, of which the first order, "somewhere" includes both the realm of common life and the realm of Stygia, while the second order, "nowhere," is the order into which the river flows, and in which life becomes meaningless and Stygia is rendered an antique fable. We may say, then, that the final rhetorical self-presentation of the poem is not that of a simple agon. The relation between "nowhere" and "somewhere" is not presented as an agon; Stygia dissolves into a nostalgic myth, the river flows naturally nowhere. It is only as we realize this that we see we had been wrong in interpreting the disappearance of Stygia in favor of the river of rivers only in an agonistic fashion. Stygia receded voluntarily, so to speak, in the light of flashing gaiety; the gaiety, we recall, had no need of dominating or striding over Stygia. Things happen as they happen; Stygia recedes or does not; the river flows or does not; eventually, when the river flows nowhere, even the familiar fable of Stygia, conceivable when we are on the brink of death but not when we actually die, will simply not exist. Over both Stygia and the river arches a single gate: "This river is fateful, like the last one."

It is by his use and yet correction of conventions such as the stream of life, Stygian banks, the agon of light and darkness, the valediction preceding death, and so on, that Stevens creates and corrects his orders of magnitude. His incessant literary reference makes the late poems extremely rich, but chiefly to those for whom his words are dense with past usage, both his own and that of other poets. Stevens' short oblique poems are rich by implication, whereas the discursive poems are more explicitly rich, even overdetermined, and consequently better understood. The style and form of Stevens' shorter poems are imperfectly seen when the poems are taken separately; the austere and pure ways by which the late Stevens presents his grandest orders of magnitude—the "somewhere" of Connecticut and Stygia, and the "nowhere" which will replace them—can be valued only against his first, apparently richer but in fact easier, simpler, or more deceptive representations of these orders. "As a man becomes familiar with his own poetry," Stevens wrote, "it becomes as obsolete for himself as for anyone else. From this it follows that one of the motives in writing is renewal . . . . One gets tired of the monotony of one's imagination, say, and sets out to find variety" (*The Irrational Element in Poetry, OP,* 220–21).

It is that variety and that renewal, that refusal to become obsolete, that strikes us as we see the style and form of the short poems changing (even in the few instances I have been able to mention here) in order to accommodate the new facts of age and death, the new perceptions of experience. Stevens' fortitude in resisting with new invention each successive washing away by magnitude is finally what we fall silent before, to "hear what he says, / The dauntless master, as he starts the human tale" (*Puella Parvula*).

NOTES

INTRODUCTION

1. Peter Brazeau, *Parts of a World: Wallace Stevens Remembered* (New York: Random House, 1983), 43.

2. *Ibid.*, 121.

3. *Ibid.*

4. Wallace Stevens, *Opus Posthumous* (New York: Knopf, 1957), 161. All future references will be given, like this one, parenthetically in the text.

5. "Romanticism and the Status of the Object," *Studies in Romanticism* 21 (Winter 1982), 555.

6. Brazeau, 290.

7. "Helen Vendler tries to make a romantic of him, bent on self-expression, so that the fantastic and wonderful 'Le Monocle de Mon Oncle' is really about the failure of his marriage!" This comment is by David Young, in " 'A Postcard from the Volcano': Gaiety of Language," *Field* 21 (Fall 1979): 29. To my mind, there is no lyric poet who does not have the aim of "self-expression," from Sappho to Ashbery. Of course, only "fantastic and wonderful" self-expression can qualify as interesting literature. But to deny that poetry is the projection of fact *(e.g.,* a failed romantic endeavor) onto the plane of language is to deny Stevens' own sense of poetry: "The real is only the base. But it is the base" *(OP,* 160). Are we not to think of Whitman's Civil War poems as about the Civil War, as well as activities of the imagination? The historical and cultural bases of poetry are important to it; it is not an exercise of disembodied "imagination."

8. Brazeau, 264–66, 282.

9. *New York Review of Books* (March 31, 1983), 10.

10. I take the reference to "that serene he had always been approaching" to be an allusion to Keats's "On First Looking into Chapman's Homer."

CHAPTER 1

This chapter first appeared in the AWP *Newsletter* (May 1979). It was subsequently reprinted in *Part of Nature, Part of Us: Modern American Poets* (Cambridge, Mass.: Harvard Univ. Press, 1980), 40–58.

Notes

1. Wallace Stevens, *The Palm at the End of the Mind* (New York: Random House, 1971), 278. Unless otherwise indicated, quotations from Stevens' poetry are drawn from this collection, and are identified parenthetically by title in the text.
2. The chinks of its prison that let through the strips of light may perhaps come from Waller's poem, *Of the Last Verses in the Book*, which seems to me also a source for Stevens' *To an Old Philosopher in Rome*. This is the close of the poem:

> The soul's dark cottage, battered and decayed,
> Lets in new light through chinks that time has made;
> Stronger by weakness, wiser men become,
> As they draw near to their eternal home.
> Leaving the old, both worlds at once they view,
> That stand upon the threshold of the new.

Cf. Stevens:

> On the threshold of heaven, the figures in the street
> Become the figures of heaven . . .

> Two parallels become one, a perspective.

> He stops upon this threshold,
> As if the design of all his words takes form
> And frame from thinking and is realized.

CHAPTER 2

1. *A Midsummer Night's Dream*, V, i.
2. Samuel Taylor Coleridge, *Complete Poetical Works*, ed. E.H. Coleridge, I, 456.
3. "Reviewing the Critics," *Parnassus* 8 (Spring, Summer, Fall, Winter 1980), 334. Beaver also remarks on what he calls Stevens' "peculiarly mincing panache, the phony francophone fuss." This is to regard Stevens' style as something applied over and above what his import requires, a view of Stevens that seems to me wholly wrong when applied to the work as a whole. Stevens' desire for absolute precision is not fuss for the sake of fuss, any more than his French words are "phony." The English language, for instance, has no word approximating to the meaning of *foyer* as Stevens uses it in *Local Objects*. The English incomprehension of Stevens continues almost unabated (Frank Kermode being the exception that proves the rule). In *Encounter* 53 (Nov. 1979), the poet Craig Raine, writing an essay in honor of Stevens' centenary, says of *The Paltry Nude Starts on a Spring Voyage* that it is "a poem about innocence eventually confronting the final experience of age. . . . The nude is, one guesses, a sailing boat. . . . Later, the

ship will be weather-beaten, a goldener nude, and will eventually sink" (66). Of course the poem is about our impoverished American Venus, who has none of the classical trappings of Botticelli's Venus, but who will eventually accumulate aura and mythological fullness through new American art.

4. See *Souvenirs and Prophecies*, by Holly Stevens (New York: Knopf, 1976), 166:

> There is my spectre,
> Pink evening moon,
> Haunting me, Caliban,
> With its Ariel tune.

5. Wallace Stevens, *Letters*, ed. Holly Stevens (New York: Knopf, 1966), henceforth identified parenthetically in the text as *L*.

6. Emily Dickinson, *Poems*, ed. Thomas H. Johnson (Cambridge, Mass.: Belknap Press of Harvard Univ. Press, 1955) II, 522.

7. *Notes toward a Supreme Fiction*, "It Must Change," II; "These are the days when Birds come back," *Poems*, I, 92. Dickinson's poem continues, "Oh fraud that cannot cheat the Bee— / Almost thy plausibility / Induces my belief." It is a Stevensian poem, and one almost certainly known to Stevens.

8. Samuel Taylor Coleridge, *Notebooks*, ed. Kathleen Coburn (New York: Pantheon Books for Bollingen Foundation, Bollingen Series L, 1957)I, 1456. 7. 9 (Aug. 1803).

CHAPTER 3

1. John Keats, *Poems*, ed. Jack Stillinger (Cambridge, Mass: Belknap Press of Harvard Univ. Press, 1978), 221. I have added the grave accents.

2. *Ibid.*, 238.

3. B.J. Leggett has called attention to the importance of Stevens' reading in "Stevens' Psychology of Reading: 'Man Carrying Thing' and Its Sources," *Wallace Stevens Journal* 6 (Fall 1982), 51–59.

4. "[In poetry] the primary relation of each word . . . is to the other words, not to the things or actions they describe." *The Practical Imagination* (New York: Harper and Row, 1983), 9. It is through these "horizontal" relations that the words in a poem are enabled to create a *gestalt*. It is this *gestalt*, and not any single word, that may then be referred to "the base" from which it has been projected. That is, the poem as a whole may be seen as referential, without its specific words being seen as referential one by one. The form of the poem is also referential, but not denotatively so; it is geometrically referential (as the familiar tragic shape of the rise and fall of the hero is geometrically referential to his fate).

Notes

CHAPTER 4

1. Ed. Whit Burnett (New York: Dial Press, 1942); rpt. Doubleday, 1970).

2. The poem is Stevens' counterstatement to Keats's nightingale ode. Keats evaded there the problem of language by representing his bird-composer as producing a song-without-words; but poetry is song-with-words, and Stevens resolves, as he so often does, to pursue a Keatsian invention one step further. Wordsworth had evaded the question of meaning by having his solitary reaper sing in Gaelic.

3. For another instance of "somnambulisma," see Stevens' *The Necessary Angel*, (New York: Vintage Books, 1951) 65: "We live in the center of a physical poetry, a geography that would be intolerable except for the non-geography that exists there."

4. "The stream of consciousness is individual; the stream of life is total. Or, the stream of consciousness is individual, the stream of life, total" *(OP,* 157). Stevens realizes, in the second of these two sentences, that the two phenomena are not parallel, as the first sentence implies. Rather, the second phenomenon incorporates the first. The aphorism, corrected, reflects Stevens' fastidiousness of phrasing, in the light of which no examination of his language, even of his punctuation, can be too minute.

INDEX

Poems by Stevens alluded to or cited.

The Hodges Lectures

ℭ

THE BETTER ENGLISH FUND was established in 1947 by John C. Hodges, Professor of English, The University of Tennessee, 1921–1962, and head of the English Department, 1941–1962, on the returns from the *Harbrace College Handbook,* of which he was the author. Over the years, it has been used to support the improvement of teaching and research in the English Department. The Hodges Lectures are intended to commemorate this wise and generous bequest.

Volumes Published

Theodore Roosevelt Among the Humorists: W.D. Howells, Mark Twain, and Mr. Dooley, by William M. Gibson

Arts on the Level: The Fall of the Elite Object, by Murray Krieger (1981)

Books and Painting: Shakespeare, Milton, and the Bible: Literary Texts and the Emergence of English Painting, by Ronald Paulson (1982)

THE HODGES LECTURES book series is set in ten-point Sabon type with two-point spacing between the lines. Sabon is also used for display. The series format was designed by Jim Billingsley. This title in the series was composed by Williams of Chattanooga, Tennessee, printed by Thomson-Shore, Inc., Dexter, Michigan, and bound by John H. Dekker & Sons, Grand Rapids, Michigan. The paper on which the book is printed bears the watermark of S.D. Warren and is designed for an effective life of at least 300 years.

THE UNIVERSITY OF TENNESSEE PRESS : KNOXVILLE